# AN ACCEPTABLE SACRIFICE?

# AN ACCEPTABLE SACRIFICE?

## Homosexuality and the Church

Edited by

DUNCAN DORMOR
AND JEREMY MORRIS

First published in Great Britain in 2007
Society for Promoting Christian Knowledge
36 Causton Street
London SW1P 4ST

British Library Cataloguing-in-Publication Data
A catalogue record for this book is available from the British Library

ISBN-13: 978-0-281-05851-8
ISBN-10: 0-281-05851-2

1 3 5 7 9 10 8 6 4 2

Typeset by Graphicraft Limited, Hong Kong

# Contents

## Part 1
## THE USE OF SCRIPTURE

## Part 2
## HISTORY AND TRADITION

## Part 3
## REASON AND PERSONHOOD

# List of contributors

Michael Beasley was appointed Chaplain of Westcott House in 2003. He is also a Research Fellow with 'The Partnership for Child Development' group based at Imperial College, London, which helps governments in the developing world establish and run school health programmes.

Malcolm Brown is Principal of the Eastern Region Ministry Course within the Cambridge Theological Federation where he teaches Christian Ethics. He is the author of *After the Market: Economics, Moral Agreement and the Churches' Mission* (2004) and (with Paul Ballard) *The Church and Economic Life – A Documentary Study: 1945 to the Present* (2006).

Arnold Browne is a former Fellow of Trinity College, Cambridge and an Honorary Fellow of Royal Holloway, University of London. He has specialized both in New Testament studies and in counselling psychology and is currently working on a commentary on the letter to the Hebrews.

Maggi Dawn is the Chaplain to Robinson College, Cambridge. She writes and teaches on hermeneutics and on the theology and practice of contemporary liturgy, and is currently working on a book on S. T. Coleridge's *Confessions of an Inquiring Spirit* (forthcoming 2007).

Duncan Dormor is Dean of St John's College, Cambridge and lectures in the Divinity Faculty on the sociology and anthropology of religion. He was the co-editor with Jack McDonald and Jeremy Caddick of *Anglicanism: The Answer to Modernity* (2003) and has written *Just Cohabiting?* (2004).

John Hare qualified in medicine in 1964. A former consultant obstetrician and gynaecologist at Hinchingbrooke Hospital, Huntingdon, he is Quondam Fellow of Hughes Hall, Cambridge and the author of over a hundred scientific papers. He was ordained priest in 2003 and works as an assistant priest in the Diocese of St Edmundsbury.

Jessica Martin has been a Fellow and College Lecturer in English Literature at Trinity College, Cambridge since 1999 and was ordained priest in 2004. She is the author of *Walton's Lives: Conformist Commemorations and the Rise of Biography* (2001). She is currently completing a life of the egyptologist, philosopher and theologian Margaret Benson (1865–1916).

Andrew Mein has been Old Testament Tutor at Westcott House, Cambridge since 1997. His main areas of interest include Old Testament ethics,

Babylonian exile and the history of the Bible's reception and interpretation. He is the author of *Ezekiel and the Ethics of Exile* (2001).

Jeremy Morris is Dean of Trinity Hall, Cambridge, where he is also Robert Runcie Fellow in Ecclesiastical History. His research and teaching interests include modern Anglican history and theology, ecumenism, and ecclesiology. Recently he co-edited, with Nicholas Sagovsky, *The Unity We Have and the Unity We Seek* (2003), and wrote *F. D. Maurice and the Crisis of Christian Authority* (2005) and *Renewed by the Word: The Bible and Christian Revival since the Reformation* (2005).

# Foreword

ARCHBISHOP EMERITUS DESMOND TUTU

*An Acceptable Sacrifice?* The answer is simple: No. It is not acceptable for us to discriminate against our brothers and sisters on the basis of sexual orientation just as it was not acceptable for discrimination to exist on the basis of skin colour under Apartheid. We cannot pick and choose where justice is concerned. And this is a matter of justice, and indeed of love. God does really loves us. Each one of us is deeply precious to him as we should be to each other. God is looking then for a society in which there are no outsiders; in which all are within and treated with respect and dignity. To treat some people as less worthy of acceptance on account of their skin colour, gender or sexual orientation brings grief to God, it is unacceptable in his sight. Let me be clear. Sexuality is part of the fullness of our humanity. Some Christians talk about it as if it were simply genital, but it is about the whole person, and to deny the richness of sexual expression to those who are homosexual is to assist in the process of their dehumanization.

I am conscious that there will be many Christians and churches in the Anglican family who will not agree with me. The 'gay debate' has brought much distress and division to our life together in the churches of Africa as well as in those of the northern hemisphere. It is for this reason therefore that I strongly commend this book as one to 'think things through' with. Its authors sincerely believe that a more accepting approach to gay Christians is compatible with the heart of the Christian faith. Yet they are scrupulous in their attempt to promote a deeper and more open conversation about the issue with those who disagree. Such a conversation is well overdue. Indeed the very future of Anglicanism depends upon it taking place. The following pages are a good place to start.

*Archbishop Emeritus Desmond Tutu*

# Introduction

DUNCAN DORMOR AND JEREMY MORRIS

The note of crisis and alarm within worldwide Anglican Christianity is inescapable. Deep divisions over the question of homosexuality run through the Anglican churches, stirred up by events in 2003, including the consecration of a practising gay bishop in the Episcopal Church in the United States, the blessing of same-sex relationships in the Anglican Church of Canada, and in the Church of England the appointment and then withdrawal of a gay candidate as Suffragan Bishop of Reading. The possibility of a permanent split has hung over the Anglican Communion since then. These divisions are not of course confined to Anglicanism. They can be found in Methodism, in churches of the Reformed and Lutheran traditions, and in Roman Catholicism. But they have perhaps never been as bitter there, or as destructive, as they have in Anglicanism. Advocates of a change in the Church's policy towards homosexuality and their opponents have traded insults and claimed the moral high ground. At least in the Church of England, somewhere between the extremes of these polarized sentiments probably lie the vast majority of churchgoers, with people uncertain what to make of it all, or people opposed to a change or supportive of it, who nevertheless do not regard it as a church-breaking issue.

Whatever the sensitivities of the silent majority in the Church, the strength of feeling aroused by the question of homosexuality in the Church forces Anglicans to face the question, Is this *the* major crisis confronting Christian faith today? It is after all a key point at which the traditional teaching of the Christian Church comes into conflict with the beliefs, values and even practice of a significant part at least of modern western society. You could put that another way, and say it is acutely symbolic of modernity's challenge to Christian faith. For more is at stake here than a question only of people's behaviour. If, when Christians argue about homosexuality and its compatibility with the Bible, they are actually arguing about homosexual practice (i.e., a sexual relationship between two people of the same gender), nevertheless their argument cannot but be affected also by contemporary understanding of what constitutes human identity – psychological, biological, social as well as moral. The modern understanding of human biology, and in particular of genetics, of the role of early years (and the closest family relationships) in psychological formation, and of the challenge and relevance of social values in relation to gender and sexual relationships – these are all matters on which the modern world has much to say that was not known, not well understood, or at least understood differently, in the past. It is not capitulating to trendy ideas to see that, nevertheless, advances in human understanding do inevitably affect the way Christians see the world. The confrontation of knowledge and Christian tradition has, of course, occurred at many points in the past – think of Copernicus, of Galileo, of the discovery of America, of the growth in understanding of disease and its treatment. Indeed when told we were co-editing a volume of essays on homosexuality, a colleague said that on this issue it was as if the Church was trying to argue that the world was still flat. And beyond this question of human knowledge, too, there is a question of a clash of values – another part of the confrontation of Christian faith and modernity. Think for example of arguments over slavery, and over women's roles and leadership, to name but two. This is not to say that simple parallels can be drawn between, for example, arguments over slavery and arguments over homosexuality. Things are more complicated than that. But it is to suggest that the argument cannot realistically be resolved by a process of moral decision-making that takes absolutely no account whatsoever of the changed situation of homosexual people today. Gay Christians are not automatically bad Christians – though we are all in need of repentance.

Much has already been written on this matter. What is the justification for yet another book? We are not writing for academics primarily, but for a more general audience, and so we are not attempting to pitch into the more complex issues of biblical interpretation at any length (though we do have things to say about the Bible). We are a group of theologians who work mostly in a university context, and in theological education. We are challenged daily to defend the practice and beliefs of the Christian Church, and to teach, but we also exercise our ministry under a sense of responsibility (not least to our colleagues) to press arguments and explore conclusions. Many of us write for an academic audience in various different theological disciplines. We are accustomed to taking time to develop arguments, to muster, analyse and assess evidence, and to move cautiously towards provisional conclusions. But here we seek to open up a wider perspective. Out of a basic belief that the Church of England should be able to move to a position of greater toleration of faithful, stable gay relationships, we want to lay out for those outside the academy, as well as within it, reasons why we believe this is a debate worth having in the Church.

It is the conviction of the authors of this volume that, for all that this is an issue on which there are serious matters of principle on both sides, and for all that the symbolic nature of the confrontation of Christian faith and modernity is very acute, this is *not* actually a decisive question for the survival of Christian faith itself, nor for the survival of the Church of England and of Anglicanism more widely. That may seem ironic, given that we are devoting a whole book to the question. But we acknowledge that there are – as we shall be arguing at various points in this book – much more pressing questions of concern to the Christian faith in our society, questions that involve the moral and physical well-being of millions of our fellow citizens, and that are in danger of being overshadowed by Anglican divisions over homosexuality. For this reason we are convinced that these divisions need not lead to schism. There are good reasons why a position that tolerates diverse practice is simply not going to work, for the issues at stake for both sides differ in weight and gravity, and what would look like an easy accommodation to one side (for example, accepting that there are many resolutely opposed to greater tolerance of homosexual practice) would look like a fundamental betrayal to the other. Yet disagreement is not going to go away. The Church of England, and the wider Anglican Communion, must be able to find a way to live with difference, and to help those who differ to take each other seriously, and not to trade abuse. If we can acknowledge a basic incompatibility between the arguments used on both sides, nevertheless we have to trust also that continued openness to each other's arguments, and continued sensitivity to the feelings of others, will eventually lead through conflict to a more reconciled and resolved position. But that new position will not entail, we argue here, a fundamental contradiction to the authority of the Bible and the teaching of the Christian tradition.

Though we share a measure of agreement on the basic question, it is by no means the case that we are all entirely agreed on the pace and nature of desirable change. It would be extremely odd were we to be so. We bring different theological perspectives to our task, different experiences and different pastoral sensibilities. But it *is* a further common conviction of ours that the gospel does in fact demand of us serious, empathetic engagement with the experience of those who struggle with the question of sexual identity and practice. Some of us have to deal pastorally with Christians who are confused or torn in two by an apparent conflict between their faith and their sexual identity and orientation. Many of us are aware of gay Christians – perhaps we should underline the point and say gay, *sexually active* Christians – who seek to lead faithful, holy lives. Indeed, in a way, that is the key issue. How can a person who is convinced that their attraction to someone of the same gender can legitimately find sexual expression within a committed, loving relationship nevertheless do so in such a way that they can lead a life of authentic Christian discipleship? Given all that we now know about sexual identity and orientation, the traditional answer – penitence and abstinence – no longer seems sufficient. There is much to be learnt from those who struggle to live with these apparent incompatibilities.

How far this is an undecided question for Christians is very difficult to determine. Despite the flood of publications advocating one view or another, there is little hard evidence of what ordinary churchgoers think about this. Our hunch – but it is no more than that – is that a large number hover uncertainly between a definite 'No' and a definite 'Yes'. Undoubtedly many are torn between a reluctance to abandon the traditional Christian view of same-sex relations, and a 'common sense' perception that what people do in the privacy of their bedrooms, in a stable relationship, is not a 'big deal'. Attitudes have changed so much on the question of homosexuality within the last twenty years or so in Britain that it is hardly surprising Christians are confused. With openly gay politicians, with gay couples featuring on lifestyle programmes, with the advance of human rights legislation to encompass sexual orientation and practice, with business's recognition of the gay market and the power of the 'pink pound', the whole context in which this argument takes place has changed. Do we think that this will all one day simply roll back the other way again? Do we think that it is only to be met with a prophetic 'No'? Is there nothing constructive to be said here, no discernment to be made between what may be good and holy within a committed, loving relationship and what is not?

For all the accusations of fudge, the current position of the Church of England is actually unequivocal. It is contained in two documents, neither of which formally should be regarded as policy documents, though in practice they have come to be treated as such. One is a motion passed by the General Synod in November 1987, which asserted that homosexual genital acts fell short of the ideal contained in the 'biblical and traditional teaching', namely that 'sexual intercourse is an act of total commitment which belongs properly within a permanent married relationship'. The other is a statement produced by the House of Bishops in 1991, called *Issues in Human Sexuality*, that denied that homosexual relationships could be regarded as parallel to heterosexual relationships. Taking these two documents together, this has amounted to a definite rejection of the sexual expression of homosexual orientation for those who are ordained, and at best a grudging recognition, out of pastoral necessity, that gay relationships exist and might be found among congregations. At the Lambeth Conference in 1998 a resolution was passed that reaffirmed the traditional view in strong – and some would say narrow – terms. It affirmed abstinence for those not called to (heterosexual) marriage, and rejected homosexual practice as incompatible with scripture. The rancorous tone of the debate made it clear that this was widely seen as an exercise in turning back the clock. The resolutions of the Lambeth Conference have no legislative force in the Church of England (or indeed in any Anglican province), and yet the facts that the Anglican bishops worldwide affirmed the resolution, and that the Church of England is an episcopally ordered church, have given it great moral force. It has become a line in the sand for many in the Church of England, referred to again and again in the furore over Jeffrey John's appointment in 2003. A document issued by the House of Bishops in 2003, *Some Issues in Human Sexuality: A Guide to the Debate*, underlines this, as it merely reiterates the position reached in the original *Issues in Human Sexuality* document of 1991. Overall, the Church of England has spent time discussing the question of homosexuality – even agonizing over it – but there is nothing in the current policy, such as it is, to suggest that there is much space for change. If anything, for gay, sexually active Anglicans in England, the situation has actually got worse over the last ten years. It has become more difficult to speak up, more difficult to be open about who you are, and more difficult for gay clergy in particular.

And yet much has been said about pastoral support for homosexual people, and about listening to their experience. In 1978, the Lambeth Conference called for 'deep and dispassionate study' of homosexuality, which would take seriously both scripture and scientific knowledge, and it encouraged dialogue with those who are gay, while affirming heterosexuality as the scriptural norm. The 1991 report, *Issues in Human Sexuality*, acknowledged that it could not be the final word on the matter. The 1998 Lambeth Conference recommitted the Anglican Communion to listening to 'the experience of homosexual persons' and called upon the Primates of the Communion and the Anglican Consultative Council (ACC) to establish a means for monitoring and sharing the work done on the question of human sexuality throughout the Communion. Little has happened on that as yet. In 2004, the Windsor Report, produced by the commission established to examine the impact of various developments including the consecration of Gene Robinson, the gay, sexually active Bishop of New Hampshire, made a similar call. Even those who are opposed to any change in the Church's policy are thus apparently committed to a process of study and listening, and to an ongoing debate. But where, when and how will debate take place, and with whom? Gay Christians might be permitted a certain scepticism about the commitment of the Church of England to debate, since little has happened to make it clear that the commitment is real.

What we offer here has a double role. First, it is partly intended as an introduction to the key questions the issue of homosexuality raises for the Church. We recognize that it is, therefore, an introduction to the terms of a conflict – and it may also be an examination of the adequacy of some of the common expressions of that conflict. It may be that some feel we have been unnecessarily cautious and oblique. There are other books that lay out directly arguments for or against, however, and little would be gained from a mere repetition of them. Rather, we have tried to ask questions about *implications*, as they might occur to people who are genuinely unresolved in what they think about homosexuality and the Church. What are the implications for our reading of the Bible? For the Church's authority? For marriage? For the relationship of Church and society? But, second, this book is also intended as an encouragement to further debate, from a group of people who, despite some differences of view, ultimately do represent a position broadly sympathetic to the pleas of gay people that the Christian Church should find a way to recognize their claim to be faithful to the gospel. We are, we hope, alert to the complexity of the question. We accept that there is a particular responsibility on us to take great care in acknowledging the honesty and witness of those who do not share our view. Many of our colleagues and friends remain opposed to the position we represent, and we value their friendship and their integrity. We recognize, too – against the carping commentary of much of the media – that the task of those (above all, the bishops) entrusted with maintaining the unity of the Church of England is not an easy one. It is no part of our aim to share in the crude disparagement of the Church's efforts to address this issue. The position of those who advocate change of any kind, especially in the context of nearly two thousand years of history, is not an enviable one. There is no consensus within the Church of England currently on the scriptural, moral and theological basis on which a change could be made, and arguing (as we do here) for a position that seeks consensus is fraught with difficulty. But the effort, we believe, must be made. The current climate of hostility and recrimination hardly helps that process. In the current situation, even those who stop short of our position, who seek some sort of 'holding' position, reaffirming the traditional position while being open to further exploration, are likely to be regarded by some as unforgivably liberal and compromised. A spirit of genuine openness has much to commend it, no matter how hard it may be in practice to sustain.

In essence we seek here to explore a position that is attentive to the authority of scripture, alert to the unity of the Church, and sensitive to the integrity and experience of practising gay Christians. That third point is of course precisely the really contentious one. Our hunch is that a large number of ordinary churchgoers basically are searching too for something like the balance of commitments we have outlined here. This is a new situation for the Church of England, and it calls for consideration of the notion of moral and doctrinal development. What is the history of a mere thirty years' or so discussion in comparison with the two thousand years of Christian history? Yet change occurs, and it is foolish – or perhaps wilfully obtuse – of Christians to ignore change. We believe there must be a prospect of hope for those who are gay, who do not think that sexual expression of their identity is a fundamental betrayal of the gospel, and who believe they can lead faithful Christian lives, and that the Church must wake up to this. As things stand at the moment, however, the Church of England is asking of gay men and women an immense sacrifice. Is it an acceptable sacrifice?

# Part 1

# THE USE OF SCRIPTURE

If the Bible is, as Christians of almost all traditions acknowledge, the foundation and supreme authority for the Church, how should we use it when we consider the question of homosexuality? Maggi Dawn opens up the basic issue of interpretation here, and challenges us to overcome the temptation to launch unreflectively into the business of swapping texts. Andrew Mein then invites us to look at the Old Testament. What is its view of sexuality? Is it straightforwardly what we would recognize as a 'conservative' position today? Arnold Browne turns then to the New Testament, and above all to St Paul, and again queries the tendency to assume that Paul's theology stands only on one side of the debate.

All these writers suggest that scripture is multi-layered, complex and full of stories and insights that sometimes sit uneasily with each other. Christians are called to a continuing conversation with the world of the biblical writers themselves in which, they argue, questions must be put to them out of the situation in which we find ourselves today. The outcome of this conversation cannot be concluded in advance. And yet it is a conversation within the one faith, inspired by the gospel of hope and salvation in Jesus Christ. That perhaps should guide the spirit of the conversation – a spirit of attentiveness and openness, a spirit of charity and sympathy – and give it a clear purpose, namely the clarification of what is God's will for us in the world. Homosexuality raises new challenges for Christians today – challenges we shall explore later in this book. But instead of simply assuming that there is no scope whatsoever for change in the Church's traditional teaching on it, and that the Bible forces us to rule any consideration of change out of court, we should consider at least the possibility that the Bible opens up for us different layers of meaning, and various imperatives, which make a positive response to those who are homosexual much more plausible than would have seemed possible just two generations ago.

# 1

# Whose text is it anyway?
# Limit and freedom in interpretation

MAGGI DAWN

All sides of the current debate concerning homosexuality and the Church appeal to scripture. This is in no way surprising, for the Bible is our holy book; as such, it is not our only source of authority, but it is a central and significant one. Yet this particular debate has so polarized opinion, not only about the interpretation of scripture, but about the consequences of disagreement, that the scriptures are in danger of being employed less as a source of life and liberty than a battering ram with which to overcome the opposing arguments.

It is easy to defend conflicting positions by arguing that two or more fundamentally different interpretations of scripture cannot be right at the same time. Red does not equal white; up does not equal down. Yet despite the seeming importance of this issue of sexuality, if it leads us to divide the Church into factions then our desire for uniformity of opinion has overtaken the prior call of the Lord to love one another. 'This is how the world will know that you are my disciples – that you love one another' (John 13.35). Christ's words were spoken not to doe-eyed teenagers united in their mission, but to a group of people all of whom had a stake in Christ's ministry and who had a record of disagreement; furthermore these words are located, in John's telling of the story, at the Last Supper, at a point when the disciples were about to come under more pressure than they ever imagined. The potential for factions between them was high, and so was the likelihood of their abandoning their common purpose under pressure. And at just that point came the call to love one another. 'By this will the world know' – know that your love for one another exceeds the pressure, keeps you together under duress, makes keeping faith with fellow believers the highest priority.

This is not to say, however, that embracing different interpretations is to deny that difference exists. The cartoon caricature of the Anglican liberal is a woolly minded thinker so concerned to be nice to everyone that he or she never gives a straight answer and answers every question with 'Well, it depends what you mean by . . .'. It is not the case that admitting the possibility of difference is to fudge the issue, or to combine differing views into an impossible and meaningless compromise. Making out that we all agree when we do not wouldn't help anyone, and it wouldn't give due respect to the painstaking work and thought that people on both sides of the argument have put into this discussion. The call to place loving one another higher on the agenda than agreeing with one another is simply an imperative of scripture – we are nowhere called to agree with each other; but we are everywhere called to treat each other with the love, care and respect due to a fellow human being. Christ's call to his disciples to love one another was not a romantic statement, but a command given to a group of people already fractured, and about to come under intense pressure. One of them was about to betray the rest; as a group they already had a history of conflict. The call to love one another is realistic and gritty – a call to stay together despite difference.

For the present debate to make any kind of constructive progress, it is probably essential to recognize that it's unlikely that we will reach a point any time soon where everyone agrees. But instead of employing the scriptures to enforce one side of the argument over another, it would do us more credit, and be more faithful to the Spirit of God, if we could recognize that a diversity of interpretation within Christianity is normal, and has a long history. My concern in this chapter, then, is to look at the whole area of biblical interpretation not with a view to endorsing one side of the argument over another, but with the aim of taking one step back from the issue at hand, and ask what it means to view scripture as authoritative when we are radically opposed in our interpretation of it.

## Historical shifts in interpretation

The first thing that may help us is to remember how significantly interpretations of scripture have shifted from one historical era to another. Over two millennia, the Church has grown through developing views of language, text, translation, reading and writing; the interpretation of scripture has changed repeatedly in the face of dramatic cultural shifts. A backward glance shows that while there are clear threads of continuity in the interpretation of the scriptures, there are at the same time examples of flexibility in interpretation, in response to cultural and intellectual shifts. One often-quoted example of an about-turn in scriptural interpretation is that of the view of slavery. At one time, various New Testament passages were taken to justify the idea that black people were destined by divine intent for slavery. Wilberforce and other members of the Clapham Sect were among those who began to rethink a biblical theology of freedom, and this new interpretation of the scriptures went hand in hand with making first the slave trade and later the owner-ship of slaves illegal. Two hundred years later, using the scriptures to support a view of subordination according to race is almost universally unacceptable.

Scientific development has also changed the way the Bible was read in relation to cosmology and human origins. Christian Europe had lived happily for fifteen hundred years with a story of the origin of the cosmos and the structure of the natural world that was uncritically assumed from the biblical narratives. But the biblical picture of a three-tiered universe with heaven above, the earth in the middle, and hell below, was gradually unpicked piece by piece as scientific discoveries from Copernicus to Darwin showed that picture of the universe and of human history to be flawed. Copernicus showed that the earth was not in the centre of the solar system. Early nineteenth-century geological discoveries began to indicate that the earth was much older than the biblical chronology suggested, eventually leading to Darwin's bombshell in 1859. But the eventual response of the Church, in each case, was not to reject the Bible in favour of science, nor to bury their heads in the sand and refuse to engage with scientific thought, but to reconsider their interpretation thus far of what the biblical texts were trying to say.

Thus we can see that significant cultural change goes hand in hand with shifts in biblical interpretation, each one causing changes in the other. In the case of slavery, a rereading of the scriptures formed part of the impetus for social change. In the case of cosmology, it was scientific development that forced a reconsideration of how the Bible was read. There are many more such instances of shifting interpretations of scripture. The Bible has been used in the past as justification for the Crusades, for corporal and capital punishment, for racism, sexism, class distinction, and the kind of treatment of children that would nowadays be considered abusive. Generations later, it is easy for us to sweep aside obsolete interpretations of scripture, many of which now seem bizarre to us, and yet to forget that we, too, are historically placed and culturally conditioned. It's easy to look back on such views and recognize that they are out of date and mistaken; yet it is equally easy to forget that at the time such views were regarded as emerging from, or reinforced by, Holy Writ. Without prejudicing the outcome, we should at least bear in mind that our current situation of conflict will, one day, be a curiosity of history. Eventually a solution will be found. But for now, we live at a time when opinion is divided. We have always believed that the Church is a worldwide body, yet we have never before been so closely and immediately acquainted with the variety of cultural interpretations.

Scientific knowledge about gender and sexuality is unfolding gradually and we do not yet know how this may lead us to review our reading of scripture. It would be more in keeping with the overarching commands of the gospel if we hold our communities together without foreclosing the debate, until that time is reached.

In the meantime, however, we need to avoid falling into the trap of viewing scripture as a means of resolving arguments to which we have set the agenda. If we are to make any progress with the issue at hand, and do so while also observing the overriding call of Christ to love one another, it is essential that we not only read the scriptures, but allow the scriptures to 'read us'. To that end, I would like to offer three ideas that might act as lenses that help to focus our view and expectation of the Bible.

## The first lens: Word and words

The first of these is that within Christian thought, the idea of 'the Word' is associated primarily not with the Bible, but with Jesus Christ, the Word of God incarnate. This idea goes back both to the Greek and the Hebrew influences upon Christianity, speaking both of the centrality of language to human experience and communication, but also of the fact that there is more to communication than words alone. One of the main narrative threads in the Bible is the idea that written words – words on a stone, on a scroll, in a book, in the mouth of a prophet – were not enough in themselves to make an effective means of communication between God and the human race. This was precisely because the purpose of such communication was not to deliver ideas, instructions, rules or commands, but to be an interpersonal communication between God and the human race. Jeremiah's account of the New Covenant (Jeremiah 31.31–34) expresses the distinction between communication of ideas and a relationship of the heart. The New Covenant, Jeremiah prophesied,

> will not be like the covenant that I made with their ancestors . . . But this is the covenant that I will make with the house of Israel after those days, says the LORD: I will put my law within them, and I will write it on their hearts; and I will be their God, and they shall be my people. No longer shall they teach one another, or say to each other, 'Know the LORD', for they shall all know me, from the least of them to the greatest, says the LORD.

Within the Christian tradition, this prophecy is connected with the accounts of the Last Supper, when Jesus says 'this is my blood of the New Covenant, which is poured out for you and for many', and its personal and incarnational quality is summed up by the writer to the Hebrews: 'Long ago God spoke to our ancestors in many and various ways by the prophets, but in these last days he has spoken to us by a Son' (Hebrews 1.1–2a).

What God communicates is not ideas or instructions, but himself. 'The Word', then, for Christians, indicates that there is a self-communication from God, not merely an exchange of information, and for this reason words alone are inadequate, and flesh-and-blood became the means through which God made himself known to us.

This complex relationship between 'the Word' and words lies at the heart of the Christian understanding of the Bible, and to read with the expectation of discerning the mind of God on any given issue is to remain alive to the complexities of this relationship. So while we owe it to ourselves and our tradition to guard and treasure a high view of the Bible, we need to avoid venerating scripture excessively, to the point where it displaces Christ the Word, and silences the capacity of Christ the Word to speak through the words on the page.

Reading the scriptures is not like trying to interpret a horoscope or read the tea leaves. We are not in the business of magic, or of fatalism. We read, not to prise knowledge from the silent gods, but in the confidence of knowing that the scriptures are a valuable but complex part of our conversation with God and with God's people. For the scriptures to do their work for us, they must be held in their true place – a secondary revelation of God. To speak of keeping the scriptures in their 'right place' is by no means to suggest a lessening of respect for the scriptures as our guide in matters of faith and conduct. Rather it is to recognize that they are part of the means through which we discern and understand God's revelation of himself to us precisely because they are a witness to Christ – the true Word of God.

In reading the scriptures, then, we are engaging with a means of listening to God whose ultimate self-revelation is not through words, but through The Word – the incarnate Christ. If ever our reading removes us from the life of Christ in favour of simple accuracy of reading, we have lost one of the central threads of what our faith is about. Such 'excessive veneration of the scriptures', as Coleridge put it, rather than making us more capable of interpreting, actually paralyses the life of the scriptures such that they become a dead word to us – a book of rules that no longer adequately connects with the realities of human existence.

The scriptures, then, are authoritative not in and of themselves, but because they bear witness to the Word of God in Jesus Christ. Yet it has proved hard for the Church to maintain this understanding. There is a human tendency to seek security, absolutes and certainty, especially at times of serious cultural change. And this tendency sometimes leads people to invest authority in the texts themselves, and to expect that the Bible will deliver up one clear and unambiguous answer to specific questions. This view of scripture walks dangerously close to treating it as a 'magic' book, or a coded message from God. For although it is a view that hopes to protect the Bible from any downgrading, the result is actually to stultify and silence the text. If we ask the text questions to which it may only give us answers on our terms – a 'yes' or a 'no' to our specific questions – then we disallow the text the capacity to speak to us in its full breadth and potential. True respect of the text demands instead that we let go of the agenda of question-asking and answer-demanding and allow the text, as it were, to read us. Letting go of the control is feared by some in case it results in a watered-down view of the scriptures, but the reality is quite the opposite, giving an understanding of the text as a dynamic tool through which we can engage with God and with one another in true, godly dialogue, thus making it possible for the scriptures to be our guide in faith and conduct without turning the Bible into a battering ram or a text to reinforce our own points of view.

## The second lens: a transparent text?

The first lens that focuses our view of scripture, then, is the fact that the revelatory capacity of the scriptures is always in the service of, and dependent upon, the revelation of God in Christ himself. The second comes from considering the nature of writing itself. What happens to texts when they are written, translated, read and reread over hundreds or even thousands of years?

The nuances of this discussion are sometimes surrounded with an anxiety that admitting to any fluidity and shift in the meaning of texts might lead to a loss of respect for the Bible as authoritative and holy. The alternative – that the scriptures are transparent and unambiguous in their meaning – is tempting in its appeal to certainty and stability, and evidently quite an easy view to adopt, as illustrated by comments in the introductory notes to some recent English translations. The *Good News Bible*, first published in 1976, was one of a number of new translations that aimed to render the Bible into accessible, everyday English. In educational terms the *Good News* required only a minimum reading age; if you could read the *Sun* or the *Mirror*, you could read the *Good News*. It was not a translation that received an unqualified welcome, as there were many who objected to the idea that the Bible could be adequately rendered into simple language. However, a more significant issue is presented by a comment in the introduction, which claims:

> The primary concern of the translators has been to provide a faithful translation of the Hebrew, Aramaic and Greek texts. Their first task was to understand correctly the meaning of the original . . . the translators' next task was to express that meaning in a manner and form easily understood by the readers . . . Every effort has been made to use language that is natural, clear, simple and unambiguous.

The transparency of meaning suggested by this comment is echoed in the cover notes of *The Message*, a paraphrase first published in 1996. It speaks of its attempt to place into contemporary language the whole Bible, from 'the mysterious stories of the Old Testament, to the straightforward language of Jesus'. Here at least there is some acknowledgement of opacity in the Old Testament texts. Yet when it comes to the words of Jesus, the language is described as 'straightforward'.

It would be mean-spirited and presumptuous to criticize contemporary translators and interpreters of the Bible for their efforts in translating the Bible into accessible language. Yet the idea that the words of scripture can be made simple and unambiguous, or that the words of Jesus are straightforward, are claims that the texts themselves do not even begin to support. The four Gospels record contradictory accounts of the words of Jesus. Within those accounts, Jesus frequently refuses to give a straight answer to a question. On some occasions, he even claimed to be obfuscating issues deliberately. The idea that the words of Jesus are straightforward, at least as we have them on record, is not a textual reality but a theological wish – a desire for there to be clarity and accessibility of meaning that the scriptures themselves do not seem either to promise or to deliver.

There are numerous instances in which the original texts could legitimately be translated in different ways, and other instances where no clear meaning is accessible at all, and the best a translator can do is to offer a 'best guess' as to the meaning. In all these cases, the translator's hunches will be informed by the theological framework he or she starts out with.

But rather than treating this as a dilemma that must be solved, it is worth recognizing that it is precisely the impossibility of nailing down once and for all a single and inflexible meaning that gives the Bible its capacity to be the means through which a living God can speak. Only a multi-layered text could give any kind of access to the God behind the words. Admitting the impossibility of precise and stable meanings is not at all the same thing as saying that we don't know what it means, or that it can mean anything we like, or that the text is meaningless. Rather it is a caution to move too swiftly to a limited range of meaning, blind to the fact that previous generations, to say nothing of present-day cultures different from our own, read and interpreted according to cultural assumptions vastly different from ours.

If we need persuading that it is possible to hold together a high view of scripture with the acknowledgement that there are multiple meanings of the texts, we need look no further than the 'gold standard' of English translations, the King James Version. As Adam Nicolson has recounted in his book *Power and Glory* (2003), the committee appointed to oversee the King James translation was selected not to narrow down single meanings, but on the basis that their diversity of church background and theological bias would guarantee that the texts would be rendered into English that deliberately included ambiguities of meaning. It is well known that, as a translation, it is by modern-day standards full of scholarly errors, which tend to be forgiven on the basis of its historical and literary value. But what is often overlooked is that the translation incorporates a variety of interpretations, embodying the sense that the authority of the text derived more from its capacity to hold differing views together than from an understanding of scripture as conveying one clear and unambiguous set of meanings. The King James Version deliberately encompassed, and even celebrated, ambiguity, and in so doing became the text to which a broad church could turn for its authority.

## The third lens: what are we doing when we read?

We have seen, then, that the Word of God is located not primarily in the text, but in the living God – Christ the Word – and that the text gains its meaning and its capacity to 'speak' through the fact that it bears witness to Christ. To say that the Bible is inspired is not to suggest that it is magically delivered to us by God, but that its authority and capacity for revelation flows from the witness it bears to Christ. So there is an intricate relationship between the ordinary human processes of writing, editing, copying and translating and the divine inspiration that gives these texts their unique revelatory capacity; it is in the relationship of the words of the text to the Word of God that this revelation is located.

Our third lens concerns the issue of what we do when we read. For if writing is not as simple and direct as it may seem, then neither is reading. Even at the most basic level of schoolroom reading, we interpret as we read. Children reading stories at bedtime or in the classroom ask questions constantly – 'Why did that happen?', 'What does that word mean?', 'If he's a "goodie", why did he do a bad thing?' And from their earliest reading children learn to interpret according to their knowledge and experience, by comparing what's happening in the story with what they already know, and with what they have read elsewhere. They learn from science books that the world has not always been the same as it is now; they learn from history books that people have not always lived, or behaved, or thought the way we do now. They learn initially from children's stories that everything will be all right in the end, but then gradually learn that there isn't always a happy ending. Set a child the challenge of writing a poem, and they immediately begin to learn that a poem has different rules of interpretation from a story. My seven-year-old son described his most recent poem to me by explaining that 'It isn't really true, you know – raindrops aren't really magic, and clouds aren't really made of feathers. But that's what it feels like.' He has already learned in infancy that the truth you find in a poem is a different sort of truth from that which deals in facts and figures. So anyone who has learned to read and write has already learned to interpret; we do so unconsciously most of the time, applying the rules of interpretation that we have imbibed from early on.

Often people seem willing to believe that certain texts, such as fiction or poetry, are subject to interpretation, whereas others, such as legal or scientific texts, are clear and fixed in their meaning. Yet not only does this not bear out in reality, it is sometimes the very opposite of the truth. A friend of mine teaches academic law. Reading the law, she says, is a matter of constant reinterpretation, for even legal texts, which aim to be as clear, unambiguous and stable as possible, are subject to constant shifts in meaning as the cultural habitat changes. The mode of expression and the cultural assumptions that guide the writing of a law give it the potential either to be misinterpreted and misapplied, or to be reinterpreted and used justly in later generations. As with law, so with sacred texts. If we assume integrity on the part of the reader, the objective in reading and interpretation is usually not to render a meaning that departs from the integrity of the text; it is to render a reading that says more clearly, more accurately in our current context, what this text was intended to mean and, in the context of a succession of cultural or geographical changes, to allow its particular interpretation to shift in order to maintain its faithfulness to the spirit of its meaning. St Paul's differentiation between the spirit and the letter of the law bears this out. To be faithful to the tradition does not mean to stay the same in the sense of preserving something in a museum; that kind of staying the same might be forensically the same, but it would change the nature of the Christian faith from something that is living and present to something that is admired and preserved, but not part of everyday life in our current context.

In addition to making the necessary allowances for interpreting across different cultures, we also have to acknowledge that there have been substantial changes in the notion of what happens when we read. The rules of reading, if you like, have changed repeatedly since the Bible was written, with varying interpretations resulting in different generations. Several factors come into play here. We have already noted that the act of translation necessarily involves a certain amount of interpretation. But the scriptures were also written in particular literary forms, many of which do not have a directly corresponding genre in later periods. Myth, poetry, history, law – all these categories have different resonances now in the West from those they carried for eight centuries BC, or in the first century AD.

## Read the text? Or be read by it?

Our Bible, then, is a collection of books, written, edited, copied and translated by human beings to record the story of salvation and to bear witness to Christ. It is also a book that, by virtue of that witness, becomes a text through which the living God continues to speak to us. And that speaking also takes account of the reader of the text – the reader's historical and cultural context; the scientific world-view of the time. What we are able to perceive of God through our reading is made possible through the inspiration of God both through writing and reading; it is also constrained by the limits of human knowledge and imagination.

In the case of the current conflict within the Church, the art of biblical interpretation offers us nothing if we employ it as trickery with words to reinforce one point of view over another. But it offers a way forward if we accept that the Bible may not answer the specific question we are asking, or it may not give us only one answer, or it may give us only a provisional and partial answer. Living with uncertainty and unclosed arguments is one of the hardest calls within Christianity. So often we want to close the deal, and settle the issue, and make things safe and certain. But this is not the way of the Spirit.

What if we deliberately set aside the lust for certainty, and anticipate the possibility that the Bible might give us multiple answers? What if we allowed for the fact that there are issues over which a clear, permanent and undisputed answer cannot be rendered from the scriptures? What if we came to the scriptures and set our questions aside? And what if we entertained the possibility that the Bible might become the location, not so much of us asking God questions, but of God gently asking of us whether we are willing to put aside the need to reconcile all views into one, and to live together with our differences?

Written contextually, and read and reread in the context of many subsequent cultures and languages, we would be foolish to pretend to ourselves that it is likely or even desirable that we will read the scriptures with precisely the same meaning they had when they were written, or at any subsequent stage in the history of the Church. Acknowledging that there is at one and the same time a core of tradition – a recognizable thread of continuity – and a margin of flexibility in application from one generation to the next, one culture to the next, is to say that we see in our faith both the stability of truth and the flexibility of a living faith. The two correct each other: the flexibility saves the tradition from becoming rigid, a museum piece with a history but no current life; the tradition maintains the corrective to the variable margins, saving the living faith from rambling anywhere without boundaries or connections to the centre.

Nowhere in Anglican history has there ever been a requirement to reach identical answers in every corner of the Church in order to have unity. It is possible to have diverging views, to disagree and still to walk together. But this uncomfortable unity is possible only by allowing the scriptures to be not an infallible and inerrant rule book, but a living, breathing body of literature through which we engage with God, and which is as likely to 'read us' as to be read by us.

To live with such difference, then, is in no way an attempt to ignore, gloss over or compromise opinion, but to walk sufficiently in humility and with a commitment to listening to the community that we continue to walk together despite substantial disagreements. We have divine permission to disagree. But we have no such permission to write one another off. We must allow ourselves a hermeneutic of difference – one that is both passionately committed to finding the answers we seek, yet prepared to admit that we see only in part; and which remains willing to respect the views – and the motives – of others, even when we find their views unpalatable. It takes humility to admit that our own reading of scripture, however valid and convincing, is still incomplete, contingent, and therefore provisional. As the Quaker adage has it, 'Allow for the fact that you might be wrong.' Christianity is both more liberating and more challenging than merely a call to team up with people who agree with us.

## Whose text is it anyway?

There is no interpretative method, nor combination of methods, that will unerringly elicit 'right answers' from the scriptures. Not because there is no truth, but because Christianity itself is not a matter of ascertaining a pure and certain set of beliefs, but of engaging with a living God. What I have proposed here is not a slippery theory that allows scripture to mean two opposing things at the same time. Rather, it is a call for enough humility to defend the interpretation you believe to be right, while still acknowledging that it may yet prove to be wrong. In so doing, it is possible to remain confident that whatever the eventual outcome, there is sufficient time and space within God's universe to see any error corrected; and sufficient grace in the heart of God to live with error. The question is, is there sufficient grace in the Church of God to wait for God's ways to be revealed? Will we be able to hold to the patient counsel and wisdom of Gamaliel? Or must we insist on a clear and pragmatic answer, no matter what the cost?

Holding different interpretations in tension, living with ambiguity of meaning, and searching for the right balance between continuity and discontinuity, do not leave us with a compromised view of scripture, but one that is, in the end, a higher view than one that insists on one, clear and unambiguous meaning. Why? Because this is a view, not of the Bible as a flat, impersonal book of rules, but of a collection of texts that connect us to a living God. With all its frustrations and difficulties, this is a view of scripture – and a walk of faith – that is a much higher calling than mere obedience to the letter.

Whose text is it anyway? Not yours. Not mine. Or, if you like, as much yours as mine. But ultimately it is not the book of the Conservatives or of the Liberals, not the book of the Gays, nor even the book of the Church, but the book of witness to the Word of God himself – Jesus Christ.

Rather than searching painstakingly for verses and passages to back up our own opinion, we must listen first and last for God's voice. In the end, if God is God, there is only one Church. If the Church does separate and go in different directions, it will not be at the call of scripture, but through the misuse of methods of interpretation to endorse one voice over another. If we walk rightly, our methods of interpretation will be undergirded by compassion, by a determination to listen carefully to others, and by the conviction that above all things we are called to love one another.

# 2

# Threat and promise:
# the Old Testament on sexuality

ANDREW MEIN

What can the Old Testament contribute to our contemporary arguments about homosexuality and the Church? For some Christians, the matter is cut and dried. Chapters 1 and 2 of Genesis, which recount the creation of the world and the creation of humankind in two rather different narratives, establish monogamous marriage between a man and a woman as the only appropriate context for a sexual relationship. Genesis 19 condemns the homosexual urges of the men of Sodom and visits upon them a terrible punishment for their immorality, namely the destruction of their city. The laws of Leviticus prohibit homosexual sex and treat it as a grave sin. The Old Testament, therefore, clearly condemns homosexuality and if we are to be faithful Christians we should pay heed to its message.

However appealing such a position might be, when we read the Bible we need to be wary of over-simple explanations. It is stating the obvious to say that the Old Testament was written more than two and a half thousand years ago in a society very different from our own. To make sense of what we find within its pages we need to put some effort into understanding the historical and cultural context out of which it came. We also need to be aware of its long history of interpretation, and of the many difficulties Christians have faced in agreeing both what it might mean and what that might imply for us.

In the case of homosexuality, our first step should be to draw a picture of sexuality and sexual relationships in the Old Testament more generally, so that we understand the context in which the material makes sense. As we do this we need to be aware of the diversity of the scriptural witness – the fact that our evidence is taken from many different books written at different periods in Israel's life. We also need to take account of the fact we no longer share many of the Old Testament's basic assumptions about the world we live in. For example, when we read Genesis 1 we discover a three-decker universe with underworld below, earth in the middle, and heavens above. The sky is conceived as a 'firmament' or dome which kept out 'the waters that were above the dome' (Genesis 1.7). This is a long way removed from a modern scientific understanding of the universe, and yet most contemporary Christians are content to recognize that the biblical writers were making the best of the knowledge available at the time. If this is the case with the physical world it should not surprise us also to find significant differences between our understanding of social and family relationships and those we find in the Old Testament, even when we use the same language. We may all support marriage and condemn adultery, but we need to dig a little deeper into the biblical world to discover whether we actually mean the same thing by these terms.

## Sexuality, commodity and control

Many aspects of the sexual morality of the Old Testament are either unfamiliar or uncomfortable for modern readers. Polygamy is acceptable, if largely restricted to the upper classes. It is also appropriate for a man to take a concubine – a slave who acts as a kind of secondary wife. There is no prohibition of prostitution, and indeed Proverbs 6.26 seems to recommend it as an alternative to adultery ('a harlot may be hired for a loaf of bread, but an adulteress stalks a man's very life').

What is surprising and striking to modern western readers is the degree to which the Old Testament understanding of sex and marriage is driven by economic concerns: sexuality and especially female sexuality is seen as a commodity. Ancient Israel was an agricultural society in which children were vital to work the land and ensure the survival of family and community. Woman's primary role was therefore as childbearer, and where questions of land and inheritance were at issue, the need for a father to know that all his children were indeed his children was paramount. What this means is that much of the material on sexuality in the Old Testament is concerned to regulate sex, to establish a hierarchical relationship that protects the rights of fathers and heads of households. Unregulated sex is a serious threat to the fabric of society. Through all of this, women's subordination to their menfolk (fathers and husbands) is a given: the system is unremittingly patriarchal.

This world of family relationships stands at a considerable distance from that of the modern West, and we need to recognize that the language of sexual relationships that we encounter in the Bible does not have the same frame of reference as in today's West. Words like 'adultery', 'rape' and even 'marriage' may therefore mean something quite different from what we expect them to. For example, we tend to assume that marriage is a contract between two equal individuals who are free to choose one another, but this is not the norm in the Old Testament (nor indeed has it been the norm for most of humanity in most places and times). For the Old Testament, marriage is an economic arrangement between two families, and a hierarchical relationship between the superior male and inferior female.

If we look at adultery in particular, Deuteronomy's law is clear: 'If a man is caught lying with the wife of another man, both of them shall die' (Deuteronomy 22.22). The crucial phrase here is 'with the wife of another man'. The woman is, in effect, her husband's property, upon which the adulterer has trespassed. The man's marital status is irrelevant. Gareth Moore emphasizes the symbolic force of sexual penetration:

> For a man to commit adultery was not for him to violate his marriage vows by having sex with another woman; it was for him to penetrate another man's wife; and that in turn meant that he treated her as his own, and so infringed the other man's property rights over her.
>
> (Moore 2003, p. 77)

The woman's crime has been to act as if she belonged to the adulterer rather than to her husband. And again, where we think of rape as a crime against the person who is raped, in Old Testament law a major concern seems to be to protect her father's investment. Deuteronomy 22.29 requires the man who is caught raping an unmarried woman to pay to her father a bride price of fifty shekels of silver, marry her, and never divorce her. This may seem an odd solution to us (not least since the daughter's wishes are of no account), but it does make the sexual relationship regular and thereby restore order.

These examples remind us that we cannot take the moral world of the Old Testament for granted as automatically parallel to our own. To understand any particular biblical injunction about sexual or family life, we need to see it in the broader historical, cultural and religious context to which it belongs. What does this imply when we turn to the texts about homosexual acts?

Perhaps the first thing to say is precisely that they are texts about homosexual acts rather than homosexual orientation. The men of Sodom (Genesis 19) or of Gibeah (Judges 19) are not 'gay' rather than 'straight'. They do seem to be gripped by a powerful sexual urge. John Barton points out that in both cases when the crowd outside the door asks for male victims they are offered female ones, and concludes that the stories 'make sense only on the assumption that sexual desire is largely indiscriminate' (Barton 1998, p. 52). But equally in these cases of attempted homosexual rape we need to ask whether the issue is not power rather than desire. The men of Sodom are attempting to express their power over Lot's visitors in the most visceral way, and they intend to do this by treating them as women.

If we turn to the laws in Leviticus – for example, Leviticus 18.22, 'You shall not lie with a male as with a woman; it is an abomination' – we find a similar situation. In the first place, it seems likely that what is condemned is anal intercourse between men rather than 'homosexuality' in a wider sense. We might want to draw a broader conclusion that if anal intercourse is outside the pale, so should be any kind of homosexual activity. However, for the time being at least it is helpful to remain with the more restricted sense, if we wish to discover what the laws might signify within the theology and world-view of the Old Testament.

Clearly Leviticus sees anal intercourse between men as a serious matter. In both cases it is described as an 'abomination', a word used to express the most severe divine displeasure. In Leviticus 20.13 ('If a man lies with a male as with a woman, both of them have committed an abomination; they shall be put to death, their blood is upon them') it appears to threaten the integrity of the community to the degree that it requires the death penalty. The text demands the same penalty for those who sacrifice children to Molech, those who curse father and mother, those who commit adultery, those who have sexual relations with their father's wife, daughter-in-law, or mother and daughter, and those who indulge in bestiality. Its presence in a list like this suggests that we need to see it within the broader context of family and religion within the Old Testament which we have already examined.

What does the prohibition imply within such a context? A number of proposals have been made. One possibility is that the main problem is one of wasted semen. The men involved have failed in their duty to perpetuate the nation, to 'be fruitful and multiply' (Genesis 1.28). Another possibility is that cultic purity is the main issue. The Old Testament makes a distinction between sin and impurity, which is difficult for modern readers to grasp. At its most basic, maintaining purity is about keeping things in their appropriate place, maintaining boundaries between different kinds of thing and person, ensuring that everything has its place within the God-given order. In this context Saul Olyan, for example, suggests that the main problem with anal sex is that it brings together two defiling substances, semen and excrement (Olyan 1994, pp. 202–3). There is an analogy here with the prohibition of sex with a menstruating woman (Leviticus 18.19), which also brings together two defiling substances, in that case semen and menstrual blood. Indeed the mixture of substances of any kind is something that Israel's priestly tradition frowns on, as can be seen from the commandments not to sow a field with two kinds of seed, or not to wear clothes made from two different kinds of cloth (Leviticus 19.19).

It is also possible that the inappropriate mixture in Leviticus 18 and 20 is of things which are too similar rather than too different: a man with a man. If this is the case, then it is highly likely that the real issue, as Robert Gagnon argues, is one of appropriate gender roles: men should be men and women should be women (Gagnon 2001, pp. 135–42). For a man to be sexually penetrated is to take on the role of a woman, and to cross a divinely ordained boundary.

Gagnon's emphasis on physiological fit seems to me to stretch the evidence too far but I believe he is right that for Leviticus the issue is fundamentally one of gender roles. However, we have seen that for men to be men and women to be women within the biblical culture carries with it a great deal of baggage about hierarchy, subordination and the idea of woman as commodity. Gareth Moore makes the point clearly in a comment on Leviticus 18.22:

> What this law depends on, and what it expresses, is the idea that God wills male superiority over the female; it also depends on and expresses a conception of sexual penetration as a symbolic actualization of the superiority. Most modern Christians reject absolutely both of these ideas, officially at least. (Moore 2003, p. 80)

It seems, therefore, that the Old Testament texts which directly address homosexual acts are not a great deal of help to us. They reflect the moral outlook of an unfamiliar and alien culture, and are thoroughly bound up with ancient Israel's broader understanding of family, sexuality and religion. If as contemporary Christians we are uncomfortable with the Old Testament's hierarchical view of sex and marriage, we may legitimately be uncomfortable with the condemnation of homosexual acts we find within it.

## Back to the beginning

If the Old Testament texts about homosexuality are largely unhelpful, where should we turn? For many Christians the issue is resolved by the opening chapters of Genesis, which have tended to shape understandings of both sexuality and the relationship between the sexes throughout Christian history. What do we find in these chapters, which deal with the origins of the world and of humanity? In Genesis 1, humanity is created male and female in God's image, and commanded to be fruitful and multiply: here sexuality seems fundamentally about procreation. In the parallel creation story in Genesis 2 we read of the woman created from the man's side and of the power of desire that leads to the unity of male and female in 'one flesh': here sexuality is about desire and the complementarity of the sexes.

Within the current Anglican debate, it is these chapters of Genesis more than any of the explicit texts about homosexuality that provide those opposed to a more affirming view of homosexuality with the core of their argument. For example, the Church of England document, *Some Issues in Human Sexuality* (2003), makes two related points: first that Genesis describes the relationship between men and women as complementary and equal, and second that Genesis 2 provides scripture's most definitive statement on the proper relationship between the sexes and sets up monogamous marriage as a kind of gold standard:

> In terms of human sexuality, this means that the description in Genesis 2 of a permanent exclusive union between one man and one woman ordained by God provides the benchmark to assess all the various forms of a sexual activity and relationship that the Old Testament describes. In so far as they do not conform to the Genesis 2 pattern, they are to be seen, like all other forms of sin, as the outworking of the fractured relationship between humanity and God described in Genesis 3.
>
> (House of Bishops Group 2003, 3.4.75)

Both of these points are open to question.

The traditional Christian interpretation of Genesis 1—2 is that it portrays not equality between men and women but a relationship of power and subordination. The man was created first (cf. 1 Timothy 2.11–15); he names the woman as he named the animals over whom he has dominion (Genesis 2.19–20), and Eve is created not as an equal but as a 'helper' (Genesis 2.18, 20), which does seem to imply inferiority. This has been the position since at least the time of Augustine, who wrote, for example, 'Nor can it be doubted, that it is more consonant with the order of nature that men should bear rule over women, than women over men' (*De Nuptiis et Concupiscientia* 1.10). Indeed for Augustine, the sole purpose of woman's creation as 'helper' appears to have been procreation:

> But if the woman were not made for the man as a helper in begetting children, for what purpose was she created as a helper. She was not to till the soil with him since there was not yet any such toil necessary. If there were such need, a male helper would have been preferable. The same thing could be said of the comfort of another's presence if, perhaps, Adam wearied of solitude. How much more agreeable for companionship in a life shared together would be two male friends rather than a man and a woman.
>
> (*De Genesi ad litteram libri duodecim* 9.5.9, quoted in Clines 1990, p. 37)

There is therefore some irony in the use of a 'revisionist' reading of Genesis to shore up a traditionalist understanding of sexuality, since the traditional view may emphasize complementarity but rarely claims equality.

It is true that some modern writers have argued, as Phyllis Trible does, that the best way of understanding the text is to see at least a glimpse of equality (Trible 1978). It is only with Genesis 3 that women become subordinate as Adam and Eve are thrown out of the Garden to begin a life of unremitting toil and painful childbirth. But this view is by no means universally shared even among recent commentators (see Clines 1990). The evidence of Adam's prior creation and naming of the woman and her role as helper is ambivalent at best.

There is also a strong case to be made that the 'plain sense' of Genesis 2.24–25 is not primarily about marriage. Genesis 2 seems to me to be much more interested in explaining sexual difference and sexual desire than social institutions. The problem that God sets out to solve at the outset is one of solitude: 'it is not good for the man to be alone' (2.18). The animals, although interesting to name, do not stir the heart and loins. But when God creates woman, a second human being, he creates the possibility of real, passionate relationship. The man responds with joy and delight: 'Now at last! . . . Bone of my bones! Flesh of my flesh!' (2.23). The emphasis is on relationship, on our need for the other, and not on either children or legal custom. Even the situation described has no basis in Israel's customs: men did not leave their parents to marry; quite the opposite happened.

In this vein, both Gerhard von Rad and Claus Westermann (perhaps the twentieth century's two most influential commentators on Genesis) argue that the story is one of the origins of the sexual drive and the need for relationship and human community, not the institution of marriage. Westermann goes so far as to say that 'the significance of the verse lies in this that in contrast to the established institutions and partly in opposition to them it points to the basic power of love between a man and a woman' (Westermann 1984, p. 233; cf. Von Rad 1961). Similarly, the more popular commentary of John Gibson sees a symbol here not of marriage but of all human relationships: 'It is the ideal symbol of a bond that ought to exist between all people the world over. God intended all humankind to be "one flesh"' (Gibson 1981, p. 119). None of these authors is an apologist for homosexual relationships, but they clearly show that marriage is not the only possible explanation for the text. Such readings seem to make sense, especially since a narrow focus on marriage in Genesis 2 can all too easily ignore the enormous difference between our twenty-first-century understandings of marriage and those of ancient Israel.

If marriage is not the culmination of Genesis 2, does it nevertheless demand that sexual relationships must be between men and women? It is true that this was the norm for ancient Israel, but must it also be the norm for us? Gareth Moore offers a creative interpretation that nevertheless takes the biblical text very seriously. His starting point is God's judgement that 'it is not good for the man to be alone' (Genesis 2.18). God is prepared to experiment in finding a solution to this problem, first by creating the animals to see if they are appropriate, and finally by offering him the woman. God does not impose any of these as a partner upon Adam, but accepts his judgement that the woman is right for him: 'The fitting partner for the man, then, is the one that he, the man, receives with joy, the one whom he himself recognizes as a partner fit for him' (Moore 2003, pp. 140–1). If Adam represents all humanity, then it is God's will for each of us to find the partner we delight in, and God will be prepared to respect our choice: 'Because God is at the service of the delight of Adam, the representative human being, then we must also suppose that he is also at the service of men whose heart is gladdened by a man and of women who delight in a woman' (Moore 2003, p. 143). Not everyone will be persuaded by Moore's argument here, but it is important to recognize that a text as rich as Genesis 1—2 will draw out interpretations as diverse as Augustine's, Westermann's and Moore's. Our responsibility as interpreters is not always to find *just one* interpretation, and one only.

Finally, while many in the Christian tradition have understood Genesis 1—2 as in some way prescriptive of human behaviour, this too is open to question. At issue is the basic genre and the aim or, as scholars put it, the 'communicative intent', of the text. Genesis 1—11 is a collection of stories about origins: most recent commentators would see its intent as to explain how and why the world is the way it is. The division of the sexes, sexual desire, and the need for companionship are all fundamental aspects of human existence which require an explanation, as do the existence of plants and animals, the pain of childbirth, and the need for agricultural labour. But it is not of the nature of this narrative, mythological literature to lay down rules for future generations. We do not insist on the basis of Genesis 2 that agricultural work is the only appropriate human labour, and many are uncomfortable with the command to dominate and subdue the earth in Genesis 1. Undoubtedly Genesis 1—11 in its canonical position serves as a kind of preface to the rest of the Pentateuch, where such themes are developed both through narrative and law. And indeed if we read it as a preface to the whole of scripture, we will find that the themes carry through into all sorts of places.

# Conclusion: two trajectories

When we approach the Old Testament as a resource for Christian think-ing about any ethical issue we are unlikely to find black and white answers. We need to pay attention to the cultural embeddedness of the texts, to the varied and often contradictory interpretations that Christians have made, and to the diversity of the biblical witness itself. As we have con-sidered the issue of sexuality we have discovered two different trajectories, or ways of thinking. Both are present within the biblical texts, and each has appealed to different interpreters.

We have seen that the Old Testament is very aware of desire and its consequences. Sexuality is a powerful force in the universe. Sexual desire contains within itself both threat and promise, both the possib-ility of real relationship and the threat of inequality and exploitation. One powerful trajectory within the Old Testament witness focuses on regulating desire. This is clear from the seventh commandment: 'you shall not commit adultery'. It is further developed through all of those laws in Exodus, Leviticus and Deuteronomy that attempt to define when and with whom it is appropriate to have sexual relations. We have seen that sexuality, and especially female sexuality, is perceived as a commodity to be traded and that sexual relationships are a way of estab-lishing dominance and control. Homosexual acts are a deeply disturb-ing aberration, in which men adopt a female role, and cross boundaries that threaten the well-being of society as a whole. We can see the roots of this trajectory in interpretations of Genesis 1—11 that emphasize male superiority and the institution of marriage.

However, there can be no doubt that the Old Testament also cele-brates sexuality. There is also a trajectory within the Old Testament that emphasizes desire and relationship. It begins with Adam's passionate cry in Genesis 2.23, and we see it most of all in the Song of Songs, a book whose poetry is unashamedly erotic, almost embarrassingly so for modern readers: 'Let him kiss me with the kisses of his mouth! For your love is better than wine' (Song 1.2). The Song is serious love poetry. It celebrates a relationship between a man and a woman that is intense, committed, passionate and consummated. It seems extraordinary that it is in the Bible at all, and even more so that it has been such a rich resource for Jewish and Christian tradition, where it has often been read allegorically as describing the relationship between God and Israel, or Christ and the Church. While the Song's original intention seems rather more earthy than this, it does suggest that through poetry like this we might learn something of God. Ellen Davis writes:

> A holistic understanding of our own humanity suggests that our religious
> capacity is linked with an awareness of our own sexuality. Fundamental

to both is a desire to transcend the confines of the self for the sake of intimacy with the other. Sexual love provides many people with their first experience of ecstasy, which literally means 'standing outside oneself'. Therefore the experience of healthy sexual desire can help us imagine what it might be to love God truly – a less 'natural' feeling for many of us especially in our secular society. (Davis 2000, p. 233)

As was the case in Genesis 2, the focus of the Song is again on passion, on relationship, on our need for the other. And with the Song it also seems unlikely that the two lovers are married. That they are deeply and exclusively committed to one another is clear, but the social institution of marriage with its attendant concerns of procreation and property could not be further from the poet's vision. This erotic poetry delights in sensuality and ignores respectable convention. Yet through it we gain a compelling vision of what it is to be human, and even what it is to be human in relation to God.

This trajectory of relationship and passion may not be as widespread as the emphasis on hierarchy and control, but it is certainly there in the biblical tradition. As we pay attention to it we begin to see the possibility that God will work through unconventional sexuality as well as conventional. With the possible exception of the story of David and Jonathan, the Bible offers no stories of homosexual relationships or positive role models for gay couples. However, texts like Genesis and the Song of Songs can help us to see that God is offering us more through the Old Testament than the rather uncomfortable picture of sexuality as commodity with which we began. There are biblical resources to imagine a different way, and to emphasize the significance of desire and reciprocity. As we now see men and women as equal partners who delight in one another, and marriage as a response to that delight, so we may begin to imagine new ways of understanding same-sex relationships as part of God's will for humanity.

# References

Barton, J., *Ethics and the Old Testament*, SCM Press, London, 1998.

Clines, D. J. A., *What Does Eve Do to Help? And Other Readerly Questions to the Old Testament*, Sheffield Academic Press, Sheffield, 1990.

Davis, E. F., *Proverbs, Ecclesiastes, and the Song of Songs. Westminster Bible Companion*, Westminster John Knox Press, Louisville, 2000.

Gagnon, R. A. F., *The Bible and Homosexual Practice: Texts and Hermeneutics*, Abingdon, Nashville, 2001.

Gibson, J. C. L., *Genesis 1—11*, Daily Study Bible, St Andrew Press, Edinburgh, 1981.

House of Bishops Group, *Some Issues in Human Sexuality: A Guide to the Debate*, Church House Publishing, London, 2003.

Moore, G., *A Question of Truth: Christianity and Homosexuality*, Continuum, London, 2003.

Olyan, S. M., '"And with a male you shall not lie down the lying of a woman": On the meaning and significance of Leviticus 18:22 and 20:13', *Journal of the History of Sexuality* 5, 1994, 179–206.

Trible, P., *God and the Rhetoric of Sexuality*, Fortress Press, Philadelphia, 1978.

von Rad, G., *Genesis: A Commentary*, Old Testament Library, SCM Press, London, 1961.

Westermann, C., *Genesis 1—11*, Continental Commentaries, SPCK, London, 1984.

# 3

# The call of Christ:
# reading the New Testament

ARNOLD BROWNE

## The light of Christ

Christians may disagree about sexuality, but they agree that they read
the Bible in order to hear and respond to Jesus Christ, the Word of
God. The very first Christian writer learned to read his Jewish scriptures in this way. Paul explained to the Corinthian congregation that
now, 'whenever Moses is read', he sees 'the light of the gospel of the
glory of Christ' (2 Corinthians 3.15—4.4). Now when he reads the
account of creation in Genesis 1—2 his focus is on Jesus: 'For it is the
God who said, "Let light shine out of darkness", who has shone in our
hearts to give the light of knowledge of the glory of God in the face
of Jesus Christ' (2 Corinthians 4.6).

Paul and his contemporaries were used to comparing different interpretations of the scriptures. They recognized that there were questions
that the text itself left open. Significantly, Paul is answering one such
question when he tells the Corinthian Christians that those who read
the scriptures in the light of Christ will not misunderstand them, that
'the veil is removed' (2 Corinthians 3.16). Paul has noticed that Exodus
34.29—35 does not say exactly why Moses put a veil on his face after
he came down from Mount Sinai. It could have been, as the Jewish
philosopher Philo suggests, because the people could not stand its
dazzling brightness (*Life of Moses* 2.70). Paul himself recognizes the
force of this argument that the people 'could not gaze at Moses' face'
because of the glory of his face (2 Corinthians 3.7). But in the story
Moses does not put on the veil until he has finished speaking to the
people. This enables Paul to give another explanation. He suggests that
Moses put on the veil 'to keep the people of Israel from gazing at the
end of the glory that was being set aside' (2 Corinthians 3.13). Paul's
answer to the question the text leaves open is that Moses put on the
veil so that the people would not see that his face ceased to shine. For
Paul, the glory of 'Moses', by which he means also the first five books

of the Bible, the Pentateuch or Torah (2 Corinthians 3.15), is fading and is to be contrasted with the lasting 'glory of Christ, who is the image of God' (2 Corinthians 4.4).

## A diversity of interpretation

Reading scripture in the light of Christ leads then to a diversity of interpretation from the beginning of Christianity. Paul's reading can differ not only from that of his fellow Jews but also of his fellow Christians. Indeed the interpretation that the glory of Moses has been 'set aside' is developed as part of his ongoing argument with other Jewish Christians. Like him they accepted Jesus as Messiah, but unlike him they wished to insist that the whole law of Moses should be binding on Gentile believers (see also Galatians 5.2–5; Philippians 3.2–4).

We find a similar diversity of Christian readings reflected in Paul's earlier letter to the congregation at Corinth. Paul finds it necessary to defend himself against fellow Christians who have questioned his apostleship. They have pointed out that he is not accompanied by a wife, as James, Peter and the other apostles are, and that, unlike them, he does not get his living by his preaching of the gospel (1 Corinthians 9.3–7). Paul acknowledges that the pattern of the other apostles' lives is based both on scripture and on the teaching of Jesus. On their side of the argument is, of course, Genesis 1—2 and the command, 'be fruitful and multiply' (Genesis 1.28). Paul agrees, as we might not, that what is written in the law of Moses – 'you shall not muzzle an ox while it is treading out the grain' (Deuteronomy 25.4) – was expressly written to give Christian apostles a 'rightful claim' on their churches (1 Corinthians 9.8–12). He acknowledges that 'the Lord commanded that those who proclaim the gospel should get their living by the gospel' (1 Corinthians 9.14), which seems to recall Jesus sending out the Twelve taking nothing for their journey (Matthew 10.5–15; Mark 6.8–11; Luke 9.2–5). And in allowing that the other apostles have the right to be accompanied by believing wives, he may also have been aware of the tradition that Jesus sent out his appointed seventy in pairs (Luke 10.1). On his own side of the argument, Paul repeatedly says that he engaged in manual labour so that he would not be a burden to those to whom he preached (1 Corinthians 9.18; 2 Corinthians 11.7; 1 Thessalonians 2.9), and he is clear that he would prefer all Christians to be single so that they can devote themselves fully to the affairs of the Lord (1 Corinthians 7.7, 32–34). Even so, Paul does not question the other apostles' interpretation of scripture or deny that they too are following Jesus. Instead he defends his own position by interpreting scripture in the light of Christ. He reads these scriptural texts not as commands that he must obey, but as rights that he has received. And, in the light of Christ, he gives up these rights to be accompanied by a wife and to be supported by the Christian community (1 Corinthians 9.12–18). For Paul this renunciation follows Christ in putting others before himself. His argument continues, 'For though I am free with respect to all, I have made myself a slave to all, so that I might win some of them' (1 Corinthians 9.19). What he says here of himself echoes the language he frequently uses of Christ, who 'emptied himself, taking the form of a slave' (Philippians 2.7).

Interpreting scripture in the light of Christ, Paul argues that it is appropriate for him to remain single and to support himself by manual labour. However, he accepts that the other apostles are being loyal to scripture and to the teaching of Jesus in being accompanied by believing wives and supported by the Christian community. Thus Paul believes that he is imitating the pattern of Jesus' life in renouncing his right to support just as much as the other apostles are following Jesus' teaching in their dependence on the community. Reading scripture in the light of Christ leads *then* not only to a diversity of interpretation but also to an acceptance of such diversity.

## The call of Christ

Since our common concern is to read the Bible in order to respond to Jesus, it is not surprising that in our current debates we are tempted to fill in the gaps where Jesus seems to be silent. Some may argue from the rigorous demands of Jesus' call, 'how hard it is to enter the kingdom of God' (Mark 10.24), that he was stricter than his contemporaries in his attitudes to sexual sin. Others may argue from his association with those despised by other religious teachers, 'this fellow welcomes sinners and eats with them' (Luke 15.2), that he was more tolerant. But it is crucial that we do not reduce the question of what it means to be faithful to the call of Jesus to a decision between strictness and leniency in the application of the law.

Already within the New Testament itself we find that there are different ways of understanding Jesus' attitude to the Jewish law. We can see this, for example, from the contrasting ways in which Matthew and Mark understand Jesus' saying that 'it is not what goes into the mouth that defiles a person, but it is what comes out of the mouth that defiles' (Matthew 15:11; see also Mark 7.15). In Matthew, Jesus' explanation of his saying to his disciples is a challenge to the Pharisees' custom of always washing their hands before eating: 'to eat with unwashed hands does not defile' (Matthew 15:20). There is no suggestion here that Jesus questioned the validity of the dietary laws contained in the Jewish scriptures themselves. However, in Mark, when Jesus explains the same saying to his disciples, 'Do you not see that whatever goes into a person from outside cannot defile?', the evangelist then adds the further explanation, 'Thus he declared all foods clean' (Mark 7.19–20). In this way Mark interprets the saying of Jesus to mean that Jesus himself set aside the scriptural dietary laws. Matthew, writing for Jewish followers of Jesus, understands him to be the Messiah who interprets and intensifies the demands of the law: 'not one letter, not one stroke of a letter, will pass from the law until all is accomplished' (Matthew 5.18). Mark, writing for Gentile followers of Jesus, shares Paul's view that in the messianic age the law itself is set aside, 'Thus he declared all foods clean' (Mark 7.20).

This diversity of Jewish and Gentile Christian readings of scripture in the light of Christ confirms that we need to move beyond the too simplistic question of whether Jesus was strict or lenient in his interpretation of the law. Instead we must ask why Jesus could be interpreted both as intensifying the demands of the law and as setting them aside. This leads us to notice that Jesus' fundamental attitude to the Mosaic regulations is to see them as inadequate. Jesus' teaching on divorce makes this point:

> Some Pharisees came, and to test him they asked, 'Is it lawful for a man to divorce his wife?' He answered them, 'What did Moses command you?' They said, 'Moses allowed a man to write a certificate of dismissal and to divorce her.' But Jesus said to them, 'Because of your hardness of heart he wrote this commandment for you. But from the beginning of creation, "God made them male and female" [quoting Genesis 1.27; 5.2]. "For this reason a man shall leave his father and mother and be joined to his wife, and the two shall become one flesh" [quoting Genesis 2.24]. "So they are no longer two, but one flesh. Therefore what God has joined together let no one separate."' (Mark 10.2–9, see also Matthew 19.3–8)

This challenge to divorce by an appeal to Genesis seems very likely to be Jesus' own teaching. Nothing Jesus says here incites anyone to disobey the law, but he does make clear that the Mosaic dispensation of commandments written 'because of your hardness of heart' is inadequate.

It is often pointed out that, in looking back to the beginning of creation, Jesus is regulating sexuality by an appeal to the creation story as affirming a model of male–female monogamy. Genesis is itself part of the law of Moses, the Torah, and so Jesus' challenge to divorce could be seen as a rigorous interpretation of the demands of the law. It is less often noticed that here Jesus is also looking forward to the new age promised through the prophets. Ezekiel had looked forward to the time when God 'will remove from your body the heart of stone and give you a heart of flesh' (Ezekiel 36.26, see also 11.19). Jesus' view that the law regulating divorce was given 'because of your hardness of heart' suggests that his teaching is for the messianic age, when hearts of stone become hearts of flesh (see also 2 Corinthians 3). In this light, Jesus' challenge to divorce could be seen to support the view that in the new age the law itself is set aside.

Once we recognize this forward-looking element in Jesus' ministry, then we may allow that his teaching on sexuality itself questions the adequacy of the Mosaic regulations, with their hierarchical framework and economic concerns (for which see the previous chapter). In challenging divorce Jesus characterizes remarriage as adultery (see Matthew 5.31–32; 19.9; Mark 10.10–12; Luke 16.18). In doing so (it is important to note) he introduces an idea not found in the Old Testament material regulating sexuality. Jesus' innovative teaching is that adultery can be committed against a woman as well as against a man: 'whoever divorces his wife and marries another commits adultery against her' (Mark 10.11; see also Matthew 19.9; Luke 16.18). Again in challenging divorce, Jesus quotes Genesis 2.24: 'a man . . . shall be joined to his wife' (see Matthew 19.5; Mark 10.7). It is worth noticing that this verse is concerned with the joy of personal companionship and the delight of physical union rather than with the command to procreate or the control of property.

## On not filling in the gaps

Jesus questions the adequacy of the law, given 'because of your hardness of heart', and his teaching on marriage emphasizes mutuality rather than dominance, relationship rather than procreation. Again this leads us to recognize that the issue facing us is not simply a matter of deciding whether Jesus was more rigorous or more tolerant than his Jewish contemporaries in his interpretation of the laws regulating sexuality. We cannot use either a supposed strictness or an assumed leniency to fill in the gaps when we find that he is silent about same-sex relationships. In Jesus' time the philosopher Philo interpreted the seventh commandment against adultery to include incest, bestiality, prostitution and a rejection of all same-sex intercourse (*On the Special Laws* 3.7–82). Certainly Jesus endorsed the commandment itself (Matthew 19.18; Mark 10.19; Luke 18.20), but that does not allow us to argue that he must have interpreted it in the same way as Philo. It is important however to notice that Jesus interprets the sin of Sodom (Genesis 19.4–11) as a failure to welcome the alien and stranger, and is silent about the sexual content of the story: 'on that day it will be more tolerable for Sodom than for that town' where 'they do not welcome you' (Luke 10.10–12; see also Matthew 10.14–15). Yet we cannot assume from this that he was therefore not opposed to homosexual intercourse. Equally his silence should make us hesitate, however, before assuming that he shared the view of those who thought the intention to penetrate men, to treat them as women, to be the worst aspect of the inhospitality. In short, the responsible course is then one of restraint, to resist conjecture and the temptation to fill in the gaps. For many such attempts are rather fanciful. For example, it has been argued that the saying in Matthew 7.6, 'Do not give what is holy to dogs', is a condemnation of homosexual relationships. The argument is that Jesus is alluding to Deuteronomy 23.18, where it is said that the wages of a male cult prostitute, in Hebrew 'a dog', should not be accepted as an offering in the house of the Lord. This does not seem very likely, since in his encounter with the Syrophoenician woman Jesus uses 'dogs' as a conventional Jewish term of abuse for non-Jews (Mark 7.24–30; Matthew 15.21–28). It might be tempting, but it would be equally fanciful, to argue that because Jesus goes on to heal the daughter of this faithful Gentile he is extending his blessing to all who are rejected as 'dogs'.

Rather than fill in the gaps with our assumptions about Jesus' strictness or leniency as a legal interpreter, we should notice instead that his ministry has a different focus. Jesus' priority is to call individuals into a community that shares his life and his destiny, proclaiming the coming of the kingdom of God in words and actions (see especially Matthew 10.5–15; Mark 6.6b–13; Luke 9.1–6). The demands of this call are more challenging than keeping any system of rules. They require more than the observance of the law of Moses, as the rich young man realized when 'he went away grieving, for he had many possessions' (Matthew 19.22; Mark 10.22; see also Luke 18.23). It is this community of disciples, those who do the will of God, who are said to be Jesus' true family (Matthew 12.46–50; Mark 3.31–35; Luke 8.19–21). It seems that Jesus' reply to the disciple who wished first to bury his father, 'Follow me, and let the dead bury their dead' (Matthew 8.21–22; Luke 9.59–60), deliberately sets the call to proclaim the kingdom of God even above the fifth commandment to honour father and mother (see also Matthew 10.34–39). Similarly, we have seen that Jesus looks back to 'the beginning of creation' to emphasize the commitment of husband and wife to one another as 'one flesh'. But we should not ignore the difficult passages in the gospel tradition which urge the priority of the call to follow Jesus as he looks forward: 'Truly I tell you, there is no one who has left house or wife or brothers or parents or children, for the sake of the kingdom of God, who will not get back very much more in this age, and in the age to come eternal life' (Luke 18.28–30; see also Matthew 19.27–30; Mark 10.28–31).

This priority of the call to hear and live the good news of the coming kingdom of God is expressed in a number of encounters where entering into a relationship with Jesus takes precedence over any application of the law of Moses. For example, the woman suffering from haemorrhages is not condemned for making Jesus unclean by her touch (see Leviticus 15.19–30), but is told by him, 'Daughter, your faith has made you well; go in peace, and be healed of your disease' (Mark 5.34; see also Matthew 9.22; Luke 8.40). In Luke 7.36–50 Jesus welcomes the kissing and anointing of his feet by a 'woman in the city, who was a sinner'. A strict interpretation of Leviticus 5.1–5 indicates a risk of defilement upon even being touched by a sinner. This is why Jesus' host says to himself, 'If this man were a prophet, he would have known who and what kind of woman this is who is touching him – that she is a sinner.' But Jesus says to him, 'her sins, which were many, have been forgiven; hence she has shown great love'. In Mark 1.40–44 (see also Matthew 8.1–4; Luke 5.12–16) the same sense of priority is seen in Jesus' touching a leper while he is still unclean (see Leviticus 13—14). Jesus himself says to the leper, 'Be made clean', even though, according to the law, it is the prerogative of the priest to pronounce a leper clean. Jesus then sends the cleansed leper to the priest to make his legal offering 'as a testimony to them'. In this way the man he has healed becomes a witness to the precedence of Jesus' saving word over any application of the law.

These encounters express clearly Jesus' sense of the inadequacy of the regulations of the law. His transgression of its boundaries between the clean and the unclean clearly horrified some of his contemporaries. However, even the law of Moses must give way to the prior claims of Jesus' call to respond to his proclamation of the coming kingdom of God. Our fundamental question should not be about his severity or tolerance as a legal interpreter. Our concern should be our faithfulness to his call to share his life and destiny.

## Imitating Christ

When we turn to consider issues relating to human sexuality it should be of no surprise, then, that the call to follow Jesus by proclaiming his gospel in word and deed is the overriding priority of the authors of the New Testament. Paul makes this very clear in his writings to the Corinthians. They have asked him whether sexual intimacy is compatible with life in Christ (1 Corinthians 7.1). In his reply Paul refers to Jesus' teaching on divorce:

> To the married I give this command – not I but the Lord – that the wife should not separate from her husband (but if she does separate, let her remain unmarried or else be reconciled to her husband), and that the husband should not divorce his wife.          (1 Corinthians 7.10–11)

Jesus taught that husbands and wives should not divorce, and Paul understands from this that sexual intimacy in marriage is consistent with Christian living. In this discussion of sexuality, Paul also follows Jesus in emphasizing mutuality rather than dominance, and passion rather than procreation. Both husband and wife are owed their 'conjugal rights'; each has 'authority' over the other's body; and the timing of intercourse is to be by 'agreement' (1 Corinthians 7.2–5). It is no sin to marry if 'passions are strong' (1 Corinthians 7.36), because 'it is better to marry than to be aflame with passion' (1 Corinthians 7.9).

In discussing sexual intimacy, Paul agrees that 'he who marries his fiancée does well', but significantly he goes on to say that 'he who refrains from marriage will do better' (1 Corinthians 7.38). Here Paul is also following Jesus in emphasizing, above all, the prior claims of the gospel. It is better for men and women to remain single. The married are concerned with 'the affairs of the world', how to please their spouses. The single can give their undivided attention to 'the affairs of the Lord, how to please the Lord' (1 Corinthians 7.31–35). The call of Jesus could demand even the leaving of a wife for the sake of the coming kingdom (Luke 18.28–30). And so, because 'the present form of this world is passing away' (1 Corinthians 7.31), Paul did not rule out separation by agreement (1 Corinthians 7.10–16), and was very clear that the single state was much to be preferred: 'I wish that all were as I myself am' (1 Corinthians 7.7).

For those whose primary concern was obedience to the law of Moses, Jews should marry only within the nation (see Numbers 25; Deuteronomy 7.1–7), although some interpreters considered marriage to Gentiles committed to joining the nation permissible. Paul, whose primary concern was the preaching of the gospel, says nothing against racial intermarriage. He considers that remaining even with an unbelieving spouse could be appropriate from the perspective of the gospel: 'Wife, for all you know, you might save your husband. Husband, for all you know, you might save your wife' (1 Corinthians 7.16). Yet again, the priority lies with the call to follow Jesus by proclaiming the gospel.

## Differing attitudes to marriage and gender

This clear emphasis on the proclamation of the gospel helps to explain what are – on the face of it – the very different attitudes to marriage found within the New Testament, and in particular the contrast between what we read in the Pastoral Letters (1 and 2 Timothy and Titus) on the one hand and in the book of Revelation on the other. The Christian community pictured in the Pastoral Letters is becoming an accepted part of society. In this context, the gospel will receive a better hearing if Christian leaders are 'well thought of by outsiders' (1 Timothy 3.7). This requires them to be men with one wife and obedient children (1 Timothy 3.2–5; 4.12). Roman society expected men to marry, and the Pastoral Letters are critical of Christians who 'forbid marriage' (1 Timothy 4.3). The Christian community pictured in Revelation is facing persecution, and it is urged to refuse to worship 'the beast' of Rome and its emperors. In this context, separation from the world and its ways is faithful witness to the gospel. In the author's vision of heaven then, it is virgins, 'those who have not defiled themselves with women', who are the true followers of the Lamb as disciples and martyrs (Revelation 14.6).

This focus on the call to follow Christ and commend the gospel in differing circumstances produces a similar tension when one considers attitudes to male and female, even when the same text (Genesis 1—2) is appealed to by a single author. So, for example, in 1 Corinthians 11 Paul uses the story of the creation of Eve from Adam's rib (Genesis 2.21–23) to argue for a hierarchical understanding of gender: 'neither was man created for the sake of woman, but woman for the sake of man' (1 Corinthians 11.8–9). That men and women were fundamentally different, and the latter subordinate to the former, was the common view of Paul's Jewish and Graeco-Roman contemporaries. This was accepted as part of the natural order. Paul can ask, 'Does not nature itself teach you that if a man wears long hair, it is degrading to him, but if a woman has long hair it is her glory?' (1 Corinthians 11.14–15). Epictetus, the Stoic philosopher, was similarly concerned with hair appropriate to each gender. Men should not shave the hair from their chins:

> Has not nature used this hair also in the most suitable manner possible? Has she not by it distinguished the male and the female? . . . For this reason we ought to preserve the signs which God has given, we ought not to throw them away, nor to confound, as much as we can, the distinctions of the sexes. (*Discourses* 1.16.9–14)

But even as Paul argues that hierarchical gender distinctions are natural, he concedes that there is another view of gender relationships: 'Nevertheless, in the Lord woman is not independent of man or man independent of woman. For just as woman came from man, so man comes through woman; but all things come from God' (1 Corinthians 11.11–12).

Thus Paul reads the Genesis story of the creation of human beings in the image of God in 'the light of the gospel of the glory of Christ, who is the image of God' (2 Corinthians 4.4). His belief that in Christ 'there is no longer male and female' (Galatians 3.28), leads him then to reread Genesis 'in the Lord' and to find not only hierarchy but also a sense of mutuality, even equality.

# A new humanity

Reading Genesis by the light of Christ prompts Paul to retell the story of Adam, the first man, in order to illuminate the significance of Christ, the last Adam: 'Thus it is written, "The first man, Adam, became a living being" [quoting Genesis 2.7]; the last Adam became a life giving spirit' (1 Corinthians 15.45). Particularly in 1 Corinthians 15 and Romans 5 he develops a series of contrasts between Adam and Christ: 'Therefore just as one man's trespass led to condemnation for all, so one man's act of righteousness leads to justification and life for all' (Romans 5.18).

It is with this contrast between Adam and Christ in mind that we approach the most important and much discussed scriptural text in the debate about same-sex relationships – Romans 1:18–32. For here, Paul looks back to give an account of human wickedness in terms of the narrative of Adam's fall (Romans 1.18–32), and forward as he argues that it is in Christ that the tragedy is reversed as men and women are 'predestined to be conformed to the image of God's Son' (Romans 8.29). In Romans 1.18–32 Paul argues that sinful humanity follows the pattern of Adam in its disordered desire to 'be like God, knowing good and evil' (Genesis 3.5). But, Paul argues, such a misplaced desire for equality with God inevitably leads to other lusts, sexual and social: 'claiming to be wise, they became fools' (Romans 1.22). Paul's argument is that these other lusts are then symptoms of God's wrath against idolatry and should be obvious to everyone, to Jews and Gentiles alike.

It was repugnant to Jews for men to be penetrated because this was for them to be treated as a woman (see Leviticus 18.22; 20.13). As women were regarded as being of an inferior nature and status, sexual acts that produced such gender confusion were to be shunned. Similarly in Roman society a male who was sexually passive was automatically effeminized. Indeed, it was a common accusation to level against an enemy. The poet Catullus attacks both Julius Caesar's authority and his masculinity when he describes his liaison with his subordinate Mamurra: 'neither one nor the other the keener seducer, chummy rivals for and of girls' (Poem 57). Thus when Paul writes that 'men, giving up natural intercourse with women, were consumed with passion for one another' (Romans 1.27), both his Jewish and his Gentile readers would have agreed that such a rejection of masculine identity is the result of rejecting God. Similarly, although there is no condemnation of female same-sex intercourse in the law of Moses, both Paul's Jewish and Gentile readers would have understood that women who 'exchanged natural intercourse for unnatural' (Romans 1.26) were rejecting their feminine identity. In Paul's time Jews had taken up the issue of female homoeroticism, and one of his contemporaries wrote: 'And let not women imitate the sexual role of men' (Pseudo-Phokylides, *Sentences* 192). In Graeco-Roman society women who loved women could be described as having 'the mind and the desires and everything else of a man' (Lucian of Samosata, *Dialogues of the Courtesans* 5.4).

Paul would have expected all his Christian readers in Rome, whether Jewish or Gentile, to see that the rejection of hierarchical gender roles, as well as 'envy, murder, strife' (Romans 1.29), undermined the foundations of human society; it provided clear evidence that 'all have sinned and fall short of the glory of God' (Romans 3.23). In Romans 1 therefore he is using the story of Adam in Genesis in the context of his proclamation of the gospel of Christ. The antithesis of Adam's selfish idolatry is Christ's selfless obedience (Romans 5.12–21). The collapse of society in Adam is reversed by the new community in Christ: 'pursue what makes for peace and for mutual upbuilding' (Romans 14.19).

Paul's reference to homosexual acts in Romans 1 is thus part of a broad theological argument concerned with the contrast between the first Adam who aspires to divinity and falls, and Christ the redeemer, the second Adam. In the context of contemporary discussion about same-sex relationships, we should notice that in this passage Paul does not use Genesis 1—3 to affirm an ideal of male–female monogamy. This is unsurprising given his view that it is the unmarried who can devote themselves fully to the affairs of the Lord (1 Corinthians 7.32–35) now that 'the night is far gone, the day is near' (Romans 13.12). When however we turn from this passage to the positive ethical instructions that Paul gives to the Christian community at Rome, the natural place for clear guidelines on behaviour, we find rather that he urges 'owe no one anything, except to love one another; for the one who loves another has fulfilled the law' (Romans 13.8). For Paul, then, 'the whole law' is summed up in the command to love your neighbour as yourself (Leviticus 19.8), and this liberates Christians from any obligation to obey 'the entire law' (see Galatians 5.2–15). As with the teaching of Jesus we find that there are gaps that are not filled in.

We must of course acknowledge that Paul's reading of Adam's fall sees homosexual acts as the reversal of 'natural' gender roles and therefore as a powerful symbol of social disorder. But, since men and women are 'predestined to be conformed to the image of God's Son' (Romans 8.29), we will wish also to consider what he has to say about the mutuality and even equality of the genders in Christ, and about social relationships in a community in which 'each of us must please our neighbour for the good purpose of building up the neighbour' (Romans 15.2). Paul characterizes homosexual desires as 'degrading passions' (Romans 1.26) and sees them as evidence of humanity's insatiable and disordered desire to be the creator rather than the creature. Yet, as we have seen, he has very positive things to say about sexual desire and union. Indeed he has more to say about passion than about procreation in allowing that sexual intimacy is consistent with life in Christ (1 Corinthians 7).

## Welcoming one another in Christ

The priority of the call to follow Jesus over any system of rules means that not all the gaps are, or indeed can be, filled in for us. That can be very uncomfortable, and from the beginning of Christianity attempts were made to find easier solutions. Jesus may have crossed boundaries between the clean and the unclean, the sacred and the profane, but some of his followers found that too shocking. In Acts 15 there is an account of a decision to impose on Gentile Christians the regulations which the law of Moses applied to resident aliens (Leviticus 17.8—18.30): 'to abstain only from things polluted by idols and from fornication and from whatever has been strangled and from blood' (Acts 15.20; see also 15.28; 21.5). The prohibition of fornication was intended to include the regulations against bestiality, incest and the penetration of males, from the passage in Leviticus 18.6–23, and abstention from 'whatever has been strangled and from blood' was intended to require of Gentile Christians that they would eat only animals slaughtered in accordance with the regulations in the same passage (Leviticus 17.3, 10–14; 19.26). The thought that a Gentile Christian should penetrate another male, or that he should eat the blood of one of God's creatures, would be equally horrific to one of those 'many thousands' of Jewish Christians, 'all zealous for the law', about whom we read in Acts 21.20.

This was not a lasting solution. In fact there is no evidence in Paul's letters that he ever agreed that Gentile Christians should observe Jewish food laws. He took the more demanding road of asking both Jewish and Gentile Christians to put their loyalty to Christ above everything else. We perhaps do not realize how remarkable it was that he could say to the Roman congregation: 'Some judge one day to be better than another, while others judge all days to be alike. Let all be fully convinced in their own minds' (Romans 14.5). After all, the observance of a special day was required by the fourth commandment: 'Remember the sabbath day, and keep it holy' (Exodus 20.8). Indeed Genesis 1—2 has more to say about the significance of the seventh day than it has about the ideal of marriage: 'So God blessed the seventh day and hallowed it, because on it God rested from all the work that he had done in creation' (Genesis 2.3).

Paul challenged those who kept the sabbath and those who did not to avoid passing judgement on each other (Romans 14.10). Instead they were to 'welcome one another, therefore, just as Christ has welcomed you, for the glory of God' (Romans 15.7). That must challenge us to be very careful of one another as we read the scriptures in the light of Christ.

## Conclusion

The call to follow Christ before all other considerations led early Christians like St Paul to see all rules, even the law of Moses, even the Ten Commandments, as being of secondary importance. So too for us wrestling with the issue of same-sex relationships. Our primary concern should be our faithfulness to Jesus' call to share his life and destiny, rather than the adoption of either a supposed strictness or an assumed leniency to fill in the gaps when we find that he is silent about same-sex relationships. Through the personal encounters with our Lord familiar to us from the Gospels, we have a powerful expression of Jesus' sense of the inadequacy of the regulations of the law. His call on our lives is more profound and challenging than the keeping of any system of rules – as the diversity of interpretation within the New Testament, in the light of differing circumstances, demonstrates. As we respond to the experience and lives of fellow disciples, brothers and sisters in Christ, who are gay, it is his voice to which we must be attentive.

# Part 2

# HISTORY AND TRADITION

How we read scripture is central to the debate in the Church about homosexuality. The Bible does not give straightforward warrant in support of active homosexual relations. Rather, the few specific texts it contains appear to criticize and condemn them, in some respects at least. But peer beneath the surface of the text, and it may not be possible simply to fall back on the argument that 'the Bible says'. Scripture must be taken seriously. But 'taking seriously' does not mean ignoring critical issues.

Get over the hurdle of biblical interpretation, and yet there is still much to settle in the matter of homosexuality and the Church. In this part, we move on to look at the question of the Church itself, and the scope within it for change. Jeremy Morris here examines the nature of the Church, and its relationship to change. Does the Church betray itself if it accepts the possibility of a change to its traditional teaching? Jessica Martin narrows the perspective down to marriage itself, a key part of the Church's teaching on sexuality, exploring the relationship between the 'institution' of marriage at the time of the English Reformation and the teachings of the Church. Finally Duncan Dormor puts this in the wider context of early modern attitudes to sexuality itself. What emerges is a complex and often surprising relationship between social mores, physical desire and Christian teaching.

Central to these essays is the perception that the Church is a historical community. Its history is relevant to our discussion, because through that history we can trace the character and the limitations of the attempts by Christians over the centuries to apply the teaching of scripture. The Church itself can change and can adapt to, and absorb, things that earlier generations might have abhorred. There is no reason to suppose that this might not also be true, one day, of a change in church policy over homosexuality. A closer examination of the history of marriage, and of sexual desire, does not disclose a fixed, static situation in which there was always one model of church marriage and, outside that, no possibility whatsoever of sexual expression, but rather a situation of changing social mores. Perhaps we are on the cusp of such a moment, when what seems inconceivable to many people today will gradually become more and more accepted as not an affront to the gospel?

# 4

# The Church and change: tradition and development

JEREMY MORRIS

Christians often suppose that once the biblical arguments about the question of homosexuality have been settled, it is easy to decide whether or not the Church should approve of a change in its traditional teaching and practice. But things are not so straightforward. How we interpret the Bible is certainly important in this debate. We cannot simply set aside its authority because we happen to disagree with some of its provisions. But there's a further series of issues, to do with how the Church lives the gospel. One of the main questions we need to examine is that of church authority, and how that relates to the messy business of human history. It is not really a matter of one or other individual's view here. Given the complexity of the issues involved in interpreting the Bible, Christians are bound to disagree among themselves on homosexuality, as well as on a range of other issues. Rather, the pertinent question is, On what basis might the *Church* decide to change its policy, given that disagreement in this area of human sexuality abounds? How close does the relationship between biblical teaching (however we determine that) and church policy really need to be?

## The nature of the Church

But before we can answer *that* question, a still more basic one rears its head. What *is* the Church? Many of the difficulties that beset Christians today over the question of homosexuality have their roots in part at least in disagreements about the nature and purpose of the Church – in what theologians call 'ecclesiology'. It would be a fearsome task to analyse and evaluate the whole range of theories about the Church to be found in the Church of England today in one short essay. My aim here is to do no more than show some of the more significant implications of the current debates for the Church of England, not by picking them out separately, but by advancing a view of the Church that highlights

49

reasons why the current arguments over homosexuality force us to confront the question about how the Church adapts to change.

In the previous section of this book, some of my fellow contributors explored the question of biblical evidence and its interpretation. It was appropriate to devote the first substantial section of this book to the Bible, as the Church of England has always recognized the prior authority of scripture. In the 'Lambeth Quadrilateral', the fourfold formula of scripture, creeds, sacraments and episcopacy, which the Anglican bishops in 1888 agreed as a basis on which Anglicans would seek union with other churches, the priority given to God's word is acknowledged by quoting the Thirty-Nine Articles (holy scripture contains 'all things necessary to salvation') and by calling it 'the rule and ultimate standard of faith'. Anglicans are agreed, then, that they stand under the authority of scripture. They have always sought to emphasize that the Church derives its authority from scripture. Article 20 ('Of the Authority of the Church') of the Thirty-Nine Articles acknowledged that the Church had 'power to decree Rites or Ceremonies, and authority in controversies of faith', but affirmed that it was not lawful for the Church 'to ordain any thing that is contrary to God's Word written, neither may it so expound one place of Scripture, that it be repugnant to another'. Strictly interpreted, this alone would destroy most modern biblical scholarship. But as we saw in the previous section, the point is that interpreting the biblical evidence is perhaps not as straightforward as some suppose. Since there are competing strands in scripture, and on the whole we are more ready to acknowledge the role of the human author and the influence of the community of interpretation (the 'audience' for scripture), it is much harder to avoid drawing out particular elements of scripture, perhaps downplaying others, than we might wish.

Nevertheless, if we begin from the apparently simple question, 'What *is* the Church?', we must seek some guidance at least from scripture. One of the most powerful metaphors for the Church used in scripture is that of a body. The application of this to a group of people united in following a leader is obvious. In the letter to the Ephesians, Paul highlights this theme of unity, speaking in passing of the body (which by implication is the body of believers): 'There is one body and one Spirit, just as you were called to the one hope of your calling, one Lord, one faith, one baptism, one God and Father of us all, who is above all and through all and in all' (Ephesians 4.4–6). Note that Paul does not directly identify the 'body' he speaks of here with the Church, but rather uses the unity that flows from the Father as the focus of the unity of faith and therefore of believers. In the letter to the Romans, Paul is more explicit: 'For as in one body we have many members, and not all the members have the same function, so we, who are many, are one body in Christ, and individually we are members one of another' (Romans 12.4–5). Here, the unity of the faithful is conceived itself as a corporate unity: the unity of believers constitutes a body which is *in* Christ. The main point of the passage is to emphasize diversity within the body. The body is not made up of people who are all exactly alike, and who are expected to perform exactly the same functions. Its variety instead echoes the variety of humankind, for in the preceding verse Paul has referred to 'the measure of faith which God has assigned [to each]' (Romans 12.3). But, Paul is saying, this individuality does not compromise the unity of the body of believers, for we are all 'individually members of one another'.

Following Paul's logic here, the unity of the followers of Christ (despite their diversity as individuals) is something corporate and collective. It is a belonging in Christ that enables us to speak of the Church as itself Christ's body. Jesus has called us to follow him. We are saved in and through his atoning death and resurrection. What makes us one is our common discipleship, which flows ultimately through Jesus Christ from the unity of God. What we mean by the word 'body' is elastic – necessarily so. In Christ's ascension, his 'body' (which, following Paul in Romans 15, we can see as not a physical body in quite the same sense as our physical bodies, but as a renewed, spiritual body) has returned to the Father, but his presence, we are assured, is also with us here on earth. His body in another sense remains on earth in the Church – and hence it is perfectly appropriate to speak of the Church as Christ's body too. We can get to the same truth by another route, namely the celebration of the Eucharist, for when Jesus said at the Last Supper, 'This is my body', and directed his disciples to do this (make this identification, this thanksgiving) in memory of him, he was in effect founding a practice which was based on a celebration of his body as present with his followers. The eucharistic community – the Church – again is his body. As we gather round the altar, and receive his body and blood in the consecrated bread and wine, we remember his body broken on the cross, and his body risen and ascended, and we share in it, and we identify ourselves with it, as a single body. That is succinctly put in the words (a paraphrase of Romans 12.5) that accompany what is technically called the 'fraction', when the priest symbolically breaks bread: 'We being many are one body, because we all share in one bread.' So there are multiple senses of 'body' at work here. The Church as Christ's body maps onto Christ's crucified, risen and ascended body: he lives in *us*. There are obvious dangers in saying directly that the Church *is* divine, since that might seem to imply that whatever the Church does automatically has divine warrant. Still, the Church has a divine foundation in the incarnation of Jesus Christ. And yet it is also a human response to Christ.

If all this sounds rather dense, what it highlights is that the Church, founded as it is on the will of Christ, has a real existence in time and space. The Church is a *moral* and *historical* community of *faith*. It is concerned above all with faithfulness to the gospel of Christ, in its following of the way of Jesus Christ. The word traditionally used to capture this sense of fidelity to the gospel is 'apostolicity'. The word, of course, is used in the Nicene Creed – 'We believe in one, holy, catholic and *apostolic* Church.' It goes hand in hand with catholicity, which means the universal character of the Church. The Church, in faithfulness to the gospel, is the same for all people everywhere, and in all time. However different you or I may be from a Christian in the fifth or the tenth or the fifteenth century, still there must be some sense in which – if we are *truly* Christian – we are held together in a universal bond of belief. The Church's faithfulness in time – its apostolicity – is protected by tradition. Now 'tradition' is an often-derided word today. When theologians and church leaders speak of tradition, they do not mean the stubborn adherence to antiquated practices for their own sake, but simply the way in which the truth of the gospel – and the Church's apostolicity – is passed (in a sense 'traded', with echoes of the Latin *traditio*, or 'handing on') from one generation to another. Tradition is not a rival authority to scripture, but the servant of the truth contained in scripture. Successive generations of Christian believers receive this tradition like a precious basket that contains the treasure of the Church's apostolicity, its faithfulness to the gospel; they hold it dear and protect it, and in turn hand it on to those who follow them.

Everything I have said so far about the Church relates to its inner identity – to that for which it stands, its spirit. But it also has a material or physical existence. The Church has an outer identity, an existence in time that enables other people to see it for what it is and to respond to it with welcome, or with hostility, or however they wish. The gospel tradition that the Church carries has to be embodied in particular ways in time and space – otherwise it would only be a theory. How is it embodied? The Church is embodied in particular institutions, buildings and places, in its ministry, and in its organization, including parishes, dioceses or districts, and so on. It is also embodied in sacraments, and especially in the sacraments of baptism and Eucharist – physical rites, which involve material things (water, bread, wine) invested with a spiritual effectiveness. The Church is also embodied in teaching, including the proper reading of scripture and its exposition in sermons. And it is embodied in the lives of those who are its members, and therefore in the life of the community of the Church itself.

For Anglicans, these aspects of the embodiment of the Church cannot ever finally be separated from each other. The sacramental reality of the Church cannot be separated altogether from the teaching of the Church, since the Church's teaching includes teaching about the sacraments. Its teaching touches on the way we live our lives, too, and so again cannot be separated from the moral life of the church community. And so we could go on.

This is the Church, then. It is something more than a collection of like-minded people. It is a unity made up of those who follow Christ, and its unity is given historical shape by particular forms of material existence. Just as we speak of our own bodies and souls, so the Church also has body and soul, both of which are willed into being by the Christ who came himself into our world as a person of flesh and blood. Just as there are illnesses of the body, there are illnesses of the soul ('sin'). The Church too can be sick in body and in spirit. The inner and outer aspects of the Church relate to each other, and when the Church is functioning well, and witnessing to the gospel, the relationship is a close and tight one.

## The Church and change

The problem with the perspective I have just outlined is that it sounds somewhat idealized and static, even making allowance for the Church's failures. It is one thing to claim that the Church as it is now is the same Church as it was in the days of the apostles. But it is quite another thing to put that claim in the context of history. We are not first-century people. The Church looks vastly different from what it was two thousand years ago. If we were going to claim that not just the spirit but the material body of the Church too must be identical to the Church of the apostles, then it would be impossible to be Christian today. There are, admittedly, many people who talk as if they think of themselves as first-century believers who happen to inhabit twenty-first-century bodies, and we can applaud the sincerity and apparent simplicity of such a view. But is it credible? Doesn't fidelity to the gospel mean something more substantial than replicating the thought-patterns of first-century people, when we no longer live first-century lives?

Let me put that question in a much more concrete perspective. Previous generations of Christians were hardly indifferent to homosexual behaviour – they were positively hostile. But then to previous generations until the late twentieth century, homosexual practice was something that stemmed from moral failure. Since there was little understanding of human sexuality as formed biologically, psychologically and socially, and yet as something which constituted a given, a centre of personality and identity for individuals, all forms of sexual behaviour were often regarded with suspicion. They were intrinsically disordered – angels would not have sex in heaven. This disordered carnal desire had to be held in place either by celibacy or by the one form of sexual relationship that Christians could regard as divinely sanctioned, namely heterosexual marriage. Can it really be argued convincingly now that our growing scientific understanding (however disputed) of the formation of the human person makes no difference whatsoever to this traditional Christian view of desire? It is right that Christian theology and ethics should not be held captive to changing scientific theory. But a change in the scope of human knowledge forces us to confront the possibility that things we once thought settled and certain are not in fact so. Is it really a betrayal of the gospel to suggest that human experience and knowledge might now lead us to think that homosexual orientation and practice is not beyond acceptance? And not contrary to the spirit of the gospel? Anglicans have tried to take account of the principle of reason in their theological method. It is perhaps a matter of reason that we should recognize that for some people homosexual orientation is not a matter of personal choice, but of inner compulsion, and that not to be able ever to express that orientation in a sexually active relationship may be (I do not say always is) not so much a choice out of Christian self-sacrifice but a crushing way of personal loneliness and despair. These arguments are not settled, for sure. There are very weighty considerations out of scripture that cannot easily be sidestepped. Since they cannot be sidestepped, we cannot but envisage continuing disagreement and argument, until such time as the Church has entered together into a new understanding of this complex matter. But there are compelling reasons to recognize that sexuality has moved into an area of contestability, in which the final outcome for the Church is not certain.

The question of homosexuality thus raises a crucial problem for the identity of the Church. What happens when the Church encounters a new situation or a new challenge, one that tradition did not seriously envisage? Can the Church change? And if it can, are we then to think that somehow the 'apostolic' tradition was mistaken? Is it – in the popular phrase – to 'have your cake and eat it'? How can the Church stay the same, and yet change? In one of the most influential discussions of this thorny problem, Cardinal Newman (1801–90), an Anglican who converted to Roman Catholicism at the age of 44, famously compared the Christian tradition to a river, with its substance unchanging but its appearance, its size, its speed, all changing as it wends its way through the countryside:

[A great idea] in time enters upon strange territory; points of controversy alter their bearing; parties rise and fall around it; dangers and hopes appear in new relations; and the old principles appear in new forms. *It changes with them in order to remain the same.* In a higher world it is otherwise, but here below to live is to change, and to be perfect is to have changed often. (my italics)

To Newman, then, the substance of the Christian faith persisted through many changes in its form and expression.

We can see this process at work in history. Sometimes the Church is pitched headlong into a changed situation. No one can foresee the consequences of the change, which may not even present themselves as fundamental issues of principle, but in time that is what they become. When the emperor Constantine 'Christianized' the Roman Empire in the fourth century, there was little direct discussion about what this new, radically altered relationship with the State might mean. But in time it began to change decisively the Church's relationship to society, and that in turn led to a gradual change in the Church's governance and order. The growth of canon law depended on this new relationship, for it presupposed stable church courts, largely free of interference. Sometimes change came about from a deterioration in the Church's own practice, and led to the tragedy of schism, a split in the Church. The 'Great Schism' of 1054 – the final separation of western, 'Latin' Christianity from eastern, 'Greek' Christianity – was the culmination of a gradual loss of charity, mutual understanding and openness in the Church. Sometimes change comes when a new interpretation of the biblical texts comes to the fore, or when a long dormant interpretation or idea is rediscovered. The Reformation was an argument over the authority of scripture, and in particular the doctrine of justification through faith alone. Sometimes change comes from altogether new information, or from developments in knowledge that at first glance do not seem much to bear on the Christian faith. The 'scientific revolution' of the sixteenth and seventeenth centuries might fall under this heading. Galileo's cosmological discoveries, reinforcing Copernicus' theory of the solar system, were a challenge to the book of Genesis. But in due course western Christianity showed itself perfectly capable of absorbing the new science.

In all these and other ways, much of what was once regarded as vital to the Christian faith has changed or disappeared. The faith the Church proclaimed has not changed in substance, centred as it is on the death and resurrection of the Lord Jesus. But to suggest the traditions of the Church have not changed at all is utterly implausible. We cannot hear and receive the book of Genesis exactly as first-century people did. Even if we reject all of modern science, and claim to accept as literally true the creation accounts in Genesis, we cannot escape doing so precisely in the full knowledge that this puts us strongly at odds with the dominant scientific account of reality – a knowledge our first-century ancestors were never forced to admit. Likewise, we cannot pretend that the Church teaches exactly what it taught in the first five centuries of the Christian era. Can we follow its view of virginity, chastity and the respective roles of men and women knowing what we do about human physiology – knowledge that was largely beyond the wildest speculation of first-century people?

But what constitutes legitimate change in the Church? Why should one kind of change not represent a fundamental betrayal of the gospel, when another kind does? Some people have tried to outline explicit criteria to evaluate legitimate developments – Cardinal Newman, quoted above, was one – but the problem with most attempts to do so is that they depend on a prior discussion of arguments that have already taken place in the Church. It is much more difficult to stretch them to accommodate a completely unforeseen development in knowledge or understanding. That problem is particularly acute in questions of sexual morality, because the rapidity with which our knowledge of human physiology and psychology has developed in the last hundred years or so has completely outpaced many of the traditional lines of Christian moral reflection. But it is important, nevertheless, to hold on to a basic distinction between what we regard as the essence of the gospel, and more secondary or derivative questions. It is often not clear whether or not something is condemned in scripture. Slavery, to use a very common example, was not explicitly condemned in the Bible (indeed it was assumed as a predictable feature of the societies of the biblical world), but in time (a long time!) Christians became convinced that it was incompatible with the message of freedom and equality before God that was basic to the gospel. Divorce did seem to be condemned explicitly, as we have seen in Arnold Browne's chapter, and yet in time many Christians began to see that marriages might fail irretrievably (and so there was a pastoral need to adapt to that), and that marriage was as much a civil institution as a religious one. Examples like this do at least show that a careful, compassionate conversation about the fundamental imperatives of the gospel might lead us to recognize even today further legitimate developments in the teaching of the Christian Church.

## Homosexuality and the Church

All of the above simply concentrates our attention all the more directly on the current arguments over homosexuality. The issue affects all of the ways in which the gospel tradition is embodied in history, from the question of whether or not gay people may be ordained, through to whether or not they should receive communion, to what the Church should or should not teach about them, and to whether, and how, they should be regarded as part of the community of faith.

This is why it is a contentious matter. It is not possible to confine the argument over homosexuality to a small part of the life of the Church, and to suggest that it is relatively trivial. Even if it is a perfectly natural reaction to think that there must be more serious and fundamental matters for the Church to address – just think of the challenge of mission in our society, for example – still the way this touches on so many aspects of the life of the Church challenges powerfully the ability of the Church to adapt and change while remaining the same. But there is a difficulty. What I have written so far has assumed that the unity of the Church is of supreme importance. The Church is a unity in time, as we have seen, marked as it is by faithfulness to the gospel (its 'internal' dimension), and by an exterior body that serves the purpose of sustaining and protecting the mission of the Church. The unity of the Church is not then a merely practical arrangement. It is not just a question of finding mechanisms or rules that will enable us to hold together – though those things are often important in themselves. The unity of the Church is a moral unity, a unity that calls us out of our particular preoccupations, our tendencies to assume egoistically that we are entirely correct, and invites us to recognize our fellowship in Christ with all those who also seek to follow him. It is a standing criticism of defensiveness, and of petty mutual suspicions. And so we cannot rest in our own inner certainty about something, even if at the same time we hold to a deep conviction that we have reached a new understanding of the implications of faith. We are bidden – if we take Christ's call to unity seriously – to interpret the unity of the Church as a unity of *charity*, a unity that holds on as much as it can to the respect and love of our fellow Christians even when we are convinced that they are profoundly wrong.

And yet the question of homosexuality does seem to strike at the very foundation of church unity. There's something asymmetrical about the arguments within the Church. The problem is that homosexuality seems to overturn the moral witness of the whole of scripture. On the traditional view, homosexual behaviour is a sin, and the Church cannot compromise with sin. In effect it is a renunciation of the gospel. On that basis there can be no compromise on the question, because any admission that Christians could afford to disagree on this matter (or rather could afford to diverge in moral practice) would be to cancel out the Church itself, to abolish the Church. This may seem to others an unduly narrow and rigid point of view, but it has of course centuries of Christian practice and belief behind it. But those in favour of a change do not regard homosexual behaviour per se as sinful (though they are willing to acknowledge that there can be many sinful forms of homosexual behaviour, just as there can be of heterosexual behaviour). They do not on the whole deny their opponents their moral legitimacy, though of course they presuppose that their own understanding is the superior one. They do plead for a broader, more generous and inclusive interpretation of scripture. But generally they presume that the argument can be sustained at a reasoned, moderate level in the Church. One side cannot compromise with a sin; the other side assumes sin is not the issue. These two positions cannot sit comfortably together. The asymmetrical nature of this agreement makes the supposition that we can all 'agree to differ' — that the model of unity we can have on this issue is one of 'reconciled diversity' — a nonsense.

Of course, the role of biblical interpretation remains vital. The argument whether or not it is right in principle for the Church to change its traditional policy on homosexuality will stand or fall, ultimately, on the possibility of elucidating a biblical basis for Christian life and practice that might include certain expressions of homosexual behaviour. Inevitably this will require a greater consensus in favour of the view that homosexual practice is not a fundamental betrayal of the gospel than appears to exist at the moment. As we have seen, in its history the Church has changed many times, while claiming to preserve unchanged the core of the apostolic faith. How has this been possible? Since the late sixteenth century, Anglican theologians have been aware that you cannot draw a blueprint for the Church from the Bible, since there are so many features of the life of the Church that need elaboration beyond the specific text of scripture. Much of what we know and treasure about the Church of England, and other Christian churches, is not directly authorized in scripture. Nor have Anglicans tied themselves closely to a specific confessional document, as have Lutheran churches to the Augsburg Confession. There are, Anglicans admit, certain authoritative documents (particularly in the Church of England) through which we receive and apply scripture — the Book of Common Prayer, the Thirty-Nine Articles of Religion, the Ordinal, for example. But we do not use these as proof-texts, since they say almost nothing about many of the controversies that have riven the Anglican churches in their more than four-hundred-year history. Yet Anglicans do reason theologically just like other churches, however, in that they do bring scripture and tradition and reason to bear on one another. They do so confessionally, out of a strong sense of what makes Anglican thinking just that, 'Anglican'. But the 'text' to which Anglicans refer is their own history. They read scripture in the light of their formularies through the history of the Church, guided by the belief that the Church is under the inspiration of the Holy

Spirit. The Church's history is not, then, theologically 'neutral'. It is the book of the acts of the faithful, and it is in the light of that text that we can discern, in the long run, the strands of continuity that hold Christians today together with those who have gone before them.

In years to come, then, Anglicans will look back on this heated controversy and ask where they should discern the true spirit of the gospel. If the Church advances further towards an inclusive view of homosexuality, will it have betrayed its vocation fundamentally, and in effect ceased to exist?

Just as there are inner and outer elements of the identity of the Church, so it displays two types of reaction to change in the world. It is as if there are two different churches. One is what I shall call the 'confessional Church'. Here, there is a basic appeal to historic, identity-forming practices and beliefs, in times of threat, when it looks as if the very existence of the Church is being called into question. The strength of this church is its loyalty to its roots. But its risk is rigidity, and an associated failure to discern where and how it might be challenged to recognize its vocation in unexpected ways – and thus it might neglect or reject those who might look to it for care. The other church I shall call the 'ecumenical Church'. This is a church that sees its identity as derived as much from a horizon of the future as from historic roots, and its decisions as provisional, open to the discernment of new or unforeseen elements of identity. Its strength, naturally, is its adaptability and expansive understanding of charity. But it too has a risk, which is a lack of substance, and a vulnerability to flimsy new theories or passing fashions. Now, it is unhelpful to pin either description on either side of the division over homosexuality, tempting though that might be. Rather, it is important to recognize the authenticity of *both*, and of the need then for *both* to be present in a rounded, authentic view of development in the Church.

In the current malaise of the Church of England over homosexuality, what this means is that the first (and in a way crucial) step is to recognize that there are important questions of Christian identity and faithfulness to the gospel on both sides of the argument. Those who oppose change in the Church are not to be blamed or written off as misguided or oppressive or stupid, just as those advocating change should not be cast as superficial or indifferent to scripture and truth, or corrupt. Both arguments have representatives and advocates who are deeply serious and committed to exploring as faithfully as they can what the gospel of Jesus Christ means for them today. The position the Church comes to in the end is most unlikely to be one that adopts only one side of the debate. If the Church is truly to show the unity to which Christ calls it, it will have to take account of the pastoral realities encountered in contemporary society, and bring the gospel to bear on those realities. And in the process it will have to grapple with the fact that the question of homosexuality concerns real people who themselves are trying to live the Christian life. Of course, as I have suggested above, both sides cannot be right at once. Finally, change in the Church must assume that one view or other will prevail. But this *is* a question of Christians arguing *together* – and staying with each other, and arguing this through in a spirit of respect and mutual care. Christians, therefore, have to explore change within the commitment to unity, since there is one Christ, and one body – however broken and beaten.

Change in the Church must occur by a way of disciplined, mutually compassionate argument, in which both sides are willing to meet those with whom they disagree, and pray and work together. In this dialectical process, a series of discoveries are likely to be made on both sides about each other's motives and experiences, and also about the problems that each has to face. For the fact is that this division over homosexuality discloses above all something obvious – that we *are* divided, and therefore different, and that we live, even as Christians in Britain, even as Anglicans, in very different kinds of communities. What looks unsurprising or normal to one group of us – namely that there are homosexual couples who regard themselves as faithful disciples of Christ – is completely beyond the experience and imagination of others. There are many church congregations in which gay couples are accepted (even if tacitly so) as fully part of the church community, just as there are many others in which such a situation is inconceivable. So this is not a theoretical argument. It is a highly practical one. It is not just a matter of deciding whether or not we will develop criteria to allow gay people to join the Church from outside, but of deciding what we are to do about acknowledging and encouraging in their Christian life those gay people who are already in the Church.

All in all, we are likely to find ourselves in the future continuing to hold to the view that the Church is a coherent, united body of followers of Christ in time, faithful to Jesus' words and work, and that there is therefore a limit to the possible diversity of the Church. That much is implied in the Christian understanding of the Church as a moral and historical community of faith. But we are also bound to acknowledge the fact that the Church is confronted here with what is really a new situation, a new context for sexual expression, in which fidelity to the gospel is to be tested and explored. The Church in its historical reality is a composite body, made up of many different kinds of community and context, in which variations of practice and value are encountered from time to time. These have to be weighed and considered in the light of the gospel. The Church's history supplies many examples of this occurring in the past. None of these are strictly comparable to the arguments over homosexuality, but in all probability none of them were strictly comparable to each other. For all that the issue of homosexual behaviour raises questions about the nature of biblical authority and its relationship to moral practice, if these questions can be resolved with mutual discernment and patience – as we argue here – there is good reason to think that the Church can absorb this change without betraying its vocation.

# 5

## Godly conversation: marriage, the companionate life and the Church of England

JESSICA MARTIN

Christians understand marriage to be at the heart of human sexual relations. Most people who accept this think it quite natural, then, to find marriage also near the centre of a Christian vision for a peaceful and ordered society. For many this is reinforced by a powerful biblical symbol of marriage at the heart of church order: Christ's relationship to his Church is understood mystically as a bridegroom's to his bride, a husband's to his wife.

The two understandings – putting Christian marriage at the heart of social stability and understanding it mystically in the relationship of Christ to his Church – seem to belong together, to reinforce each other. Theologies based around them are powerful and influential, apparently seamless. But they are, in this particular form, a relatively recent – even local – phenomenon in the story of Christianity. Once upon a time the phrase 'bride of Christ' would have evoked the image of a celibate, and in society at large marriage itself would have been much less important than virginity. And – not coincidentally – once upon a time religious celibacy could also open the door to power, riches and political influence. These were Britain's theological and social assumptions five hundred years ago, in 1500, when worldly and Christian values intertwined in every part of living. By then Christianity the world over had worked with the virginity model, in different guises, for almost a millennium and a half.

So why did it change? And were all the people who came before just wrong? Unless we just say that they were – which involves dismissing the views of quite a number of people, including St Paul and the Church Fathers to a man – we have to start wondering whether our 'natural' views about marriage are part of a theological *development* over time rather than being simply self-evident. This section looks at what changed in England in the years after 1500 to try to discern how much our current debates about sexuality, as they relate to marriage and the companionate life, are shaped by our own history. In this way we can begin to distinguish what is really fundamental to Christian living from what is customary. At the same time the insights of the last half-millennium have enriched our understanding of what the companionate life, under God, might be; we might also start to recognize the emergence of a vital mystical understanding of the nature and witness of exclusive, faithful and monogamous sexual relationships in the modern Church.

Marriage was socially important in Britain in 1500. Because the country was governed by landed families (and a monarch) whose power descended through their children, marriage mattered politically as an instrument for inheritance of goods, land and influence. It was a practical, male-dominated system; monogamy was a matter of real importance for wives, because it was the only way – before DNA testing – for a landed man to ensure that the babies born to his marriage were the true biological descendants intended to take over his position at his death. Babies were the point of marriage. Male babies were preferred (your name could only be safeguarded through your male descendants, because women took their husbands' names), though female babies could be used as bargaining points to make advantageous matches which might bring together adjacent lands, or make useful political links with other powerful families. Incidentally, an important side-effect of this concentration on reproduction was that some relationships which might in modern terms be considered sexual were curiously hard to see. For example, in a society where bed-sharing was commonplace, we cannot know how many of the women who shared beds with each other did so for deeper reasons than the warmth it guaranteed.

None of these marital arrangements had much to do with religion – though, this being Christendom, religion sanctioned every match. But the structures of the Church itself had nothing to do with marriage. Clergy, from the highest to the lowest, were celibate – although the celibacy requirement had been established comparatively late, it was now firmly entrenched. The Church was also very powerful, and a great owner of goods and lands. In England, there was an annual levy, payable from the monarch to the pope, called 'First Fruits and Tenths'; the pope was, of course, head of the English Church. Most areas had their local monastery, abbey or convent, which was the great landowner, employer and welfare system for their area. These were not always popular: the great Abbey at Bury St Edmunds had definitely got too big for its boots by 1500, and was cordially hated by the townspeople. When it was dissolved by Henry VIII in the 1530s, most ordinary folk were nothing but glad. Today it is just a few ruined walls in the middle of the municipal park.

These systems of power and wealth had nothing, of course, to do with inheritance; they were owned by the institution, that is, by the

Church. But by 1500 a fair few people were beginning to mutter that Christian living wasn't supposed to mean living in the lap of luxury and getting everyone else to do your dirty work for you (as life had become in a few of the larger monasteries); or wandering from place to place, like the mendicant friars, begging and being a public nuisance instead of earning your keep. Not all celibates kept their vows. No celibate could be *seen* to keep them – except negatively, in the sense that no child had apparently been born to them. The social status claimed by churchpeople was also sometimes resented; what had happened to Christian humility? And so on. It is difficult now to know how many of these discontents represented large-scale abuse of the system, because (as we will see) later they were all taken up and used as propaganda against the Roman Catholic Church and its structures. Dirty stories about what monks and nuns got up to after bedtime were a staple of anti-Catholic smear campaigns for centuries. 'Celibacy' even became a covert way of indicating sexual licence and was routinely contrasted with the chastity, sexual containment and social stability characterized by marriage. It is certainly the case that (sexual licence aside) entering a convent was almost the only route by which a small number of upper-class women could gain power, learning and some degree of autonomy within an all-female community, thus avoiding being helpless bargaining counters for their families' dynastic ambitions.

What about marriage for ordinary people in the towns and villages? As you went down the social scale marriage continued to be an instrument for inheritance, and so also operated to safeguard female chastity and to reduce the difficult (and widespread) problems of bastardy. But of course the fewer the lands and goods involved, the less this mattered. So legalities surrounding marriages were quite relaxed for most ordinary people. Betrothals, or 'handfastings', as they were sometimes called, although legally binding, didn't need witnesses (though witnesses were naturally felt to be highly desirable by the courts trying disputed cases): the couple pledged themselves to each other. If the case came to court it was one person's word against another's. This could matter a lot for a woman, as a reasonable percentage of couples had sex on the strength of the betrothal, and if the man went back on his agreement the woman might well have the shame of a bastard child and no means of support. In luckier circumstances, pregnancy could well be what finished the courting process and moved the couple on to actually getting married. It was – if you were a woman – a gamble for stability, with high stakes. The usual reason for breaking a betrothal was to do with worldly goods – if, for example, the woman turned out to have less to bring to a marriage than the man had hoped for. On the other hand, if you *were* poor, pregnancy might be what brought your man up to scratch, and therefore looked worth the risk.

Marriage was a sacrament – one of the seven sacraments. But, although the priest presided, the sacrament was made between the two participants, with the priest as witness. It was the words they said, not the words he said, which were efficacious. (Betrothals often used word for word the promises of the marriage service.) Marriages did not take place in the body of the church, but at the church door – which gives us some sense of how involved the Church was in the process. That is, it was as involved as it was in all the great universal rites of passage – in birth and death – thus far and no further. Indeed you could say marriage was less important than either birth or death; it was not just unnecessary to salvation (whereas baptism and extreme unction, the rite of anointing at the point of death, were both vital) but actually rather low status in the spirituality stakes. A nun was closer to God than a married woman, any day; a monk or friar than a married man; a pope than a king. That's why Thomas à Becket was so venerated – because he had made the right choice, he had put his Church before his king.

Thirty years later, all this changed – because of a famous marriage breakdown. Henry VIII, King of England since 1509, had no male heir from his now aging wife, Catherine of Aragon, and moreover had his eye on a beautiful young woman of evangelical sympathies (what we would now call Protestant sympathies) called Anne Boleyn. Catherine was well connected to Spain, and the pope, unwilling to alienate powerful allies, refused to grant a dispensation for Henry to annul his marriage. (Papal dispensations were at that time the only means for bringing a marriage to an end unless you could prove your wife to be an adulteress.) On the back of this refusal Henry climbed on the Reformers' bandwagon, declaring the Church bloated, corrupt and self-serving, and in need of returning to the pure principles of early Christianity. He stopped paying the 'First fruits and tenths' to the pope's representative, keeping the money for himself instead, declared himself Supreme Head of the Church of England, and dissolved the nation's monasteries, pocketing most of the enormous revenue they commanded to fill up his own – somewhat depleted – bank balance. He declared his marriage to Catherine null and void, without the pope's sanction, and married Anne. He also, as it happened, opened the door to clergy marriage – his own Archbishop of Canterbury, Thomas Cranmer, was a married man. The great symbolic power of celibacy was broken.

What replaced it? You'd think that the English Reformation, founded as it was on the breaking of the tie between husband and wife, wouldn't have reinforced the spiritual status of marriage much. And there were some signs that way. When the sacraments were revised down from seven to two, marriage was not one of them – because it was not necessary to salvation, whereas baptism and the Eucharist (the two which survived) were. But Henry, though not especially talented at loving and honouring specific wives, was keen on marriage. He asked his archbishop, Cranmer, whether it might be allowed to stay a sacrament, but Cranmer pointed out that that would mean that you *had* to be married to get to heaven, which was absurd. Henry reluctantly agreed (MacCulloch 1996, p. 212). If marriage had been the only requirement, his salvation would have been assured indeed.

All the same, marriage was creeping up towards being the spiritual centre of Christian living – for various reasons. One was the Europe-wide campaign among its opponents to discredit the celibate system upon which the Roman Catholic Church was based, sometimes conducted through accusations of monetary corruption, but more often and more scurrilously through insinuations of the wicked uncontrolled sexual licence enjoyed by celibates. Here is Erasmus setting the ball rolling in his famous colloquy of the 1520s, 'A Fish Diet', an imaginary conversation between a fishmonger and a butcher which ridiculed automatic religious observance divorced from moral thoughtfulness. The fishmonger is illustrating his point with a 'naughty nuns' story about foolish religious priorities:

> *Fishmonger*: During dinner . . . nobody behaved more loosely than those two [nuns] who refused to eat dinner unless prayers were said according to the use of their order. After dinner came games, dances, songs, and other things I don't dare mention; but I'm very much afraid what was done that night was hardly virginal, unless the preliminaries, the wanton games, nods, and kisses, deceived me.
> *Butcher*: I don't so much blame the nuns for that waywardness as I do the priests in charge of them.                   (Erasmus 1997, p. 707)

Erasmus never supported a break with Rome and wrote hoping for reform from within the Church. Later writers would labour the point with less humour and more malice as the political positions hardened after 1530.

Marriage, by contrast with celibacy, was seen as a controllable vehicle for sexual expression as well as being socially stable. That is to say, it was supposed to ensure fewer bastards, but it also marked out the area in which sexual activity of any kind was sanctioned. In insisting that children were a marriage's main point, it made the relatively low status of mutual sexual enjoyment very plain while at the same time insisting that sexual activity within marriage would go far to regulate lust which would otherwise find less controlled, less visible and more disturbing outlets. 'If it be the sin of Onan', wrote the Caroline divine Matthew Griffith in pragmatic mode in 1633, 'it is called pollution; if between man and man, it is called sodomitry, etc. But call it what you will, and be it what it can, marriage is a lawful and useful way of avoiding it' (quoted in Cressy 1997, p. 297).

Marriage had also become identified with government – of the State and of the Church – because the Supreme Head of both was a married man, and now the ultimate power of the Church was going to descend, via marriage, in a hereditary line. Books began to appear which deliberately used familial models to describe the peaceful, godly Commonwealth – very like today's 'headship' models in their arguments. 'He is deemed worthy to rule a Common-wealth', write John Dod and Robert Cleaver in their much read *Godly Form of Household Government* of 1603, 'that with wisdom, discretion and judgement, doth rule and govern his own house . . . none will think or believe that he is able to be ruler, or to keep peace and quietness in the Town or City, who cannot live peaceably in his own house, where he is not only a ruler, but a King, and Lord of all' (Dod and Cleaver 1603, pp. 178–9). For Matthew Griffith, marriage was not only a 'divine and spiritual, but a civil and politic conjunction' (quoted in Cressy 1997, p. 295). Elizabeth I's refusal to marry caused alarm and despondency, and contributed to the instability of the Stuart regime which followed – ultimately, perhaps, to the Civil War. It's no accident that secular marriages, not witnessed by clergy, only became possible for the first time in the republican Commonwealth – the first time that England had also managed without a monarch as its head. Marriage's spiritual and political dimensions, the association of marriage as an institution with the familial model of monarchical spiritual government, were closely intertwined.

From the reign of Elizabeth I 'privy contracts' (betrothals without witnesses) were increasingly frowned upon. Marriages themselves were conducted inside churches, and no longer at the door. The mode of the ceremony, and the ecclesiastical safeguards surrounding it, tightened. This was a part of the move towards greater ecclesiastical control of social behaviour which characterized the Elizabethan (and post-Elizabethan) state Church. As well as this, marriage's spiritual importance was emphasized so strongly that people might be forgiven for thinking it was still a sacrament. This persisted beyond 1700, receiving some reinforcement in the mid-nineteenth century. I have in my possession an early twentieth-century copy of Mrs Humphry Ward's 1888 bestseller *Robert Elsmere*, and in the margin of a discussion on marriage someone has written indignantly, in pencil, 'but marriage is a sacrament of the Church of England!' It isn't, not formally – but the anonymous writer is not the first, or the last, to make the assumption. Yet in point of fact it had replaced its sacramental status with a powerful legal one; the Church was taking seriously its job of social regulation.

This is the situation which Shakespeare explores in his problematic play *Measure for Measure* (written probably around 1608), where he presents his troubled audience with the different demands of legal justice and of unconditional mercy. Another way of putting this would be to say that he contrasts the administrative and legal aspects of state religion with the abundance of grace pouring from the heart of Christ's life and death in the Gospels. The dilemmas of the plot are these. An aristocratic couple, Claudio and Julia, betrothed and fully intending to marry, anticipate the pleasures of their wedding night by some months, and Julia is pregnant. The state where they live, Vienna (which uncannily resembles seventeenth-century London), has been getting a bit lax with its sexual mores, and it's decided to make them an example. Claudio is condemned to death by a new-broom deputy, Angelo, for transgressing an almost-obsolete state law about sexual continence. Yet Angelo himself, keen though he is, isn't as squeaky clean as he looks; there's a broken-off betrothal in his past – the girl, Mariana, hadn't got enough money in her dowry and he got cold feet. Then when Claudio's sister Isabella, about to become a nun, appeals for her brother's life, Angelo finds himself lusting after her enough to propose a devil's bargain to her: he'll pardon her brother if she'll sleep with him. She says no. (When Claudio protests at her refusal, Isabella retorts with some justice that he makes an unexpected pimp.) The plot contortions which follow are unimportant here, but some of their aspects are worth noting. First, why, in a city heaving with brothels, does Angelo decide to punish a couple who intended to marry anyway? Shakespeare explores the role of the representative of a paternal state, where the ruler is God's deputy, in relationship to the breach of a law which, *in itself*, was relatively unimportant. It's true that he's told to by his superior, the Duke, who operates as a kind of God-figure in this play, as well as a *deus ex machina* who sorts everything out in the end. But the rigours of the law are applied to the letter of marital continence, not to its spirit: the act of marrying itself, it is implied, is the only legitimate licence for mutual bodily pleasure.

So far so apparently clear. But when the Duke solves the problem, he does so by substituting the jilted Mariana for the chaste Isabella in Angelo's bed. In *that* instance, it seems, it's OK to anticipate the wedding night – because the betrothal was lawful. In fact he seems to be saying that the betrothal – probably made with the words of the marriage service – was so binding that Angelo's attempts to get out of it by claiming, legalistically, that Mariana's family hadn't provided the amount of dowry agreed (a common reason for breach of promise) were null and void, and the situation was almost as if they were married already. Mariana herself clearly understands her status as that of a wife, and pleads for Angelo's life as a wife, for better for worse. The words she says are one of the few points of pure, unconditional love the play contains: 'I crave no other nor no better man.' In the end the Duke puts aside retributive justice altogether in favour of almost universal pardon: Claudio's life is saved and he marries his Julia; Angelo marries his Mariana; and the Duke – our God-monarch – proposes marriage to Isabella, the nun-elect. She makes no answer. The ambiguous status of celibacy versus marriage as a state religious vehicle could not be more sharply drawn – just as the play itself exposes the problems which arise when a religion based on grace and mercy becomes yoked to state systems of social control. Is marriage about mutuality and vulnerability, as the wronged Mariana believes; or is it just a system for the efficient passing-on of lands and goods, as Angelo, in refusing her for an insufficient dowry and in condemning Claudio for extra-marital sex which might imperil the clear legitimacy of his heirs, appears to think? Can sex – can physical love – be regulated in this way? Throughout the play, which considers these matters from an implicitly theological viewpoint, we witness events which appear to demonstrate that it cannot.

Although children were seen as marriage's primary point, there had been another important change at the Reformation: the conscious modelling of marriage as a basis for a loving spiritual and physical partnership. This was a German import. When Cranmer was revising the wedding service he asked the advice of his friend Martin Bucer, who suggested a third reason for matrimony to go into the wedding service, along with the procreation of children and the avoidance of fornication: 'the mutual society, help and comfort which the one ought to have of the other'. This companionate model for marriage was new; implicitly, it was a very different kind of reason for tying the knot from the other two, which were negative (that's to say, they averted evils) and practical. Cranmer would have liked to have put it first, but settled in the end for it coming third (MacCulloch 1996, p. 421). All the same, its introduction was extremely important, laying a foundation for seeing marriage as modelling the ideal relationship – between man and woman, God and his people, Christ and his Church, a man and his family, a monarch and his country. In these related models the egalitarian mutuality of companionate love was becoming blended with a hierarchy based on obedience. Together they made a powerful alloy. They also, for the first time, made explicit an assumption that physical bonds might have an important spiritual aspect – and raised therefore the converse possibility, that spiritual bonds might well have a physical aspect. Married love and intimate friendship moved closer together than ever before; but they remained within their hierarchical frame.

One person on whom this blend had a very strong influence was John Milton: we see its fruits in his depiction of Adam and Eve's relationship in *Paradise Lost*, published first in 1667/68. Their love before the Fall is mutual and sensual; it is based on verbal and physical interchange rooted in respect and recognition. At the same time Adam is Eve's 'Sole Author and Disposer' (to use her words); in the famous phrase, Adam is 'for God only', Eve 'for God in him'. The hierarchy is still explicit. Even though Milton had little sympathy for the conformist understanding of God's will as exclusively filtered through the monarch, father of his people and head of the Church, the authoritarian familial point was fully alive for him, only a little mutated.

But in Milton's sense of marriage as primarily companionate lay the foundation of modern divorce. More than twenty years before writing *Paradise Lost*, in 1643, Milton published a tract called *The Doctrine and Discipline of Divorce*. In it he argued that the question of whether a couple had had sex or not was comparatively unimportant – that physical sex, being just a matter of 'outward things', should give way to the much more important question of spiritual, 'inward' compatibility. In that 'inward' communion, which he called 'conversation', lay the real bond of marriage. What, he cried, could be worse or more against God's will than to be yoked to 'a mute and spiritless mate' (Milton 1643, p. 9)? The foundation of modern 'incompatibility' pleas was thus laid on the basis of an analogical reading of Romans 3.28–29, where physical sex and actual circumcision are given the same kind of value.

This is not the place to discuss the rights and wrongs of divorce law, or to defend or attack Milton's ingenious use of exegesis. I use the example of Milton only to point up the extent to which, by the mid-seventeenth century, spiritual companionship and mental compatibility had become central to a religious view of marriage. This is a trend which has only intensified in the years which have followed, until modern views, including those held by Christians, take it as axiomatic that healthy marriages are primarily companionate. Children and their legitimacy, and the avoidance of fornication, are subordinate reasons. They are about social stability rather than being at the heart of what the marriage *is*. Few couples would cite openly as their *main* reason for being married the availability of God-licensed sex (though St Paul was less timorous than that). And what reasonable or decent person would dream of defining a childless marriage as less 'real' than one which had produced offspring? But we are all in agreement that a non-companionate marriage has something fundamental missing. Christian marriage has become the place for 'godly conversation' – physical and spiritual; it has undergone a gradual transformation into a pilgrimage for two, each learning the discipline of the other, which powerfully models the larger pilgrimage which is the Christian life, faithfully lived.

It is true that biblical understandings of marriage as a system for inheritance and the bringing-up of children have had a lot to do with how it's turned out. But is that 'Christian'? Monogamy, as it is applied to *women's* sexual activity, is chiefly useful in establishing inheritance questions. That's the practical reason why the Old Testament is completely intolerant of women taking more than one sexual partner but really pretty relaxed about men doing so. And of course all this works better when women are defined as inferior to men – indeed it relies upon it. But in themselves these assumptions don't form the backbone of Christian living in quite the way we're sometimes told they do – they have a lot more to do with social expectations which are really quite secular: the transfer of worldly goods down the generations and the relative public status of different persons (women in relation to men, children in relation to adults). There's not much about this sort of thing in the Gospels, except as examples of stuff we should not value (worldly goods) or positions we should actively oppose (the social inferiority of some categories of human being in relation to others). Jesus had strong views about the importance of women, children, the poor and the marginalised – and he took and developed these views from strong counter-cultural trends within Judaism itself, reminders running through all the Bible, from Genesis onwards, about the unique value of *all persons* created in the image of God. Companionate marriage receives these values, distilled into the giving and receiving, the interdependent demands and liberties of the monogamous relationship of two persons.

This high vision, with its ancient roots, has grown and developed with the aid of the Holy Spirit over the last five hundred years. But we are not yet at the Second Coming. The Spirit's workings are dynamic, never static, and the job of each generation, including our own, is to discern these new workings in our own time and our own context. I cannot see what these new workings will grow into, but some aspects of where we have come from may help us to take our next step. In the meantime we live with a situation which has a number of immediate injustices and a good deal of illogic, and we need to do something about it as thoughtfully and as swiftly as we may. Some tentative observations on this line follow.

Christians live with this ideal of marriage – which may have grown out of secular historical pressures, but is not itself bound or defined by those pressures, any more than Christianity itself is fully bound by its context in time and space. But once you have an understanding of a primary sexual relationship which thinks of physical intimacy in a spiritual way and of spiritual intimacy as being intertwined with physicality, then your new logic inexorably extends outside the heterosexual marriage bond towards *all* exclusive, companionate relationships and hallows them. It might be that 'godly conversation' between two persons, regardless of gender, might claim the status of marriage. Or perhaps that is not a right naming; maybe marriage is more fundamentally about children and social placings than we comfortably acknowledge. The area is a difficult one. But one injustice does seem very clear: if you privilege the question of gender above that of the companionate ideal, then you discover the situation the Church is currently in, where faithful same-sex companionate relationships are condemned as fiercely as casual sexual encounters would be, and more fiercely than casual heterosexual encounters are. This is just plain wrong.

Clearly this is a difficult area. But the question needs a proper consideration; and it is not a question of 'tolerance'. As Tom Paine points out in *The Rights of Man*, 'Tolerance is not the *opposite* of Intolerance, but is the *counterfeit* of it. Both are despotisms. One assumes to itself the right of withholding Liberty of Conscience, the other of granting it' (Paine 1984, p. 85). No Christian is in the position of assuming either.

We inherit a mystical understanding of the exclusive sexual relationship we call marriage, received through the image of Christ as Bridegroom to his Church. This model transcends worldly goods and social status; and, while it uses gender symbolically, it is not obviously gender-specific: not every member of Christ's Church is female, yet the Church is symbolically understood as a female entity. Marriage itself is more earthbound than that vision; in heaven, Jesus tells us, we will neither marry nor be given in marriage. He recognized the social and worldly roots of the question he was being asked (Matthew 22.30; Mark 12.25; Luke 20.35), and was swift to free perfected relationships from those secular bonds.

Marriage cannot be more than an imperfect vehicle within which some may strive towards the joy of perfected relationships; of true 'godly conversation'; and it seems unlikely that it is the only such vehicle. But this mystical understanding of it properly deepens what looks like just a convenient system for keeping society stable by keeping top dogs on top and making sure everyone knows their place. Monogamy is more than a safeguard against bastardy; an exclusive, intimate relationship with one other person through adult life is a journey in recognition and endurance, a training in love against the odds. Such a journey makes for a potent symbol of the enduring love of Christ for his people – also against the odds. In that sense the companionate ideal may indeed be the Christian heart of love, transforming the raw material of sexual expression into something richer and more strange. We might wish, therefore, to pause before declaring that the gifts won from the difficult business of faithful and exclusive sexual living are sanctified only in heterosexual relationships. We might even with profit wonder who 'we' are to make such judgements, who profess and proclaim Christ crucified to all.

# References

Cressy, D., *Birth, Marriage and Death: Ritual, Religion and the Life Cycle in Tudor and Stuart England*, Oxford University Press, Oxford, 1997.

Dod, John and Cleaver, Robert, *Godly Form of Household Government for the Ordering of Private Families, According to the Direction of Gods Word . . .* , Thomas Creede for Thomas Man, London, 1603.

Erasmus, Desiderius, *Colloquies*, tr. C. R. Thompson in *Collected Works of Erasmus*, 66 vols, University of Toronto Press, Toronto and London, 1997, vol. 40.

MacCulloch, D., *Thomas Cranmer*, Yale University Press, New Haven and London, 1996.

Milton, John, *The Doctrine and Discipline of Divorce . . .* , T. P. and M. S., London, 1643.

Paine, Thomas, *The Rights of Man* (first pub. 1791), Penguin Books, Harmondsworth, 1984.

# 6

# Friends, companions and bedfellows: sexuality and social change

DUNCAN DORMOR

## Introduction

'The past is a foreign country: they do things differently there.' The opening of L. P. Hartley's novel *The Go-Between* (1953) is born of the narrator's sense of the distance that exists within one individual's experience as he looks back on the events of childhood from the viewpoint of old age and reinterprets their significance. The words are often quoted, with good cause, to capture one of the central problems of history: the opaque quality of the past. At a first, naive glance, we often think we know what happened, what the 'story' is, yet the further we probe, the more we realize that the past is a world lost to us for we struggle to grasp the significance or meaning of what we first thought were 'facts'.

The past is opaque because we cannot grasp a sense of the whole, a sense of the context by which we may evaluate the significance of the parts. But it is also opaque because of our own limited capacities to see and imagine, because we bring a particular set of questions and expect a certain shape to the answers. Such pre-formed expectations often obscure our view, and nowhere is this truer than in the consideration of relationships of affection and intimacy between persons – within marriage, family and friendships. For it is here, ironically, buoyed up by the confidence and knowledge of our own personal experiences, that as we peer into the foggy past (for the emotional and sexual lives of our predecessors do not leave very reliable marks on the pages of history), we are most convinced that we see something familiar. Conversely, we can also move too quickly to dismiss the significance of past prescriptions which seem strange to us over a range of areas relating to such relationships (for example wifely deference, the physical disciplining of children, rules about sexual abstinence or even sexual positions within marriage) without fully appreciating that for our Christian forebears many of these prescriptions were regarded as of the essence of true religion.

74

Yet the past matters. It matters for society as a whole – for the present is built upon it. It matters, for a greater understanding of the past can help to bring some sense of perspective, and liberate us from the claustrophobia of the present and its preoccupations. It matters especially to the Church, for it is a communion of saints through the ages, and thus our thinking should be shaped in that wider company.

I have suggested that a consideration of the area with which we are presently concerned – that is, the world of physical intimacy, friendship and love – is fraught with difficulties. I am, then, painfully aware that what follows is not 'the truth, the whole truth and nothing but the truth' – rather it is an offering of some thoughts for further consideration. In particular I hope to cast a little light on two difficult questions which are asked much less frequently than they might be, namely: Why is it only now that same-sex relationships pose such a pressing challenge to the Christian tradition? And, why is the issue causing such turmoil in the Christian community? What is it about same-sex relationships that generates such energy, and in places, such vitriol?

In attempting to answer these questions, I want to touch on three developments over the last few hundred years that have shaped who we are, and how we experience ourselves and others. These are in broad terms: the changing character of friendship in the early modern period; the question of social order and the threats to it; and the impact of the acceptance of family limitation and contraception, over the last one hundred years, on our understanding of marriage.

## Acts and identities

One of the difficulties that plagues much of the current discussion about same-sex relationships is that of establishing *exactly* what we are talking about. At its most reductive, much of the current debate seems to be concerned with particular sexual acts, at least if they occur between individuals of the same sex. However, it is abundantly clear that the discussion runs deeper. Mature Christian reflection simply cannot boil down to an absurd adolescent game of 'how far can you go?'

What 'counts' as sex in different times and places is highly variable. What really matters then is the meaning and significance that acts carry in the wider context of ideas about personal identity, relationships and broader moral and social obligations. To give a brief example, the cardinal sexual sin within the Old Testament is adultery, understood as sexual intercourse with another man's wife, for women were regarded as a form of property and thus such an act was then an offence against the husband, therefore corrosive of social order. By contrast, the rape of a virgin, as Deuteronomy 22.28–29 (see p. 24 above) makes clear, was considered a much lesser offence, not against the woman, but against her father to whom compensation should be paid; the woman was then married off to the rapist. In our society, where individuals are understood to own their own bodies, such a solution would be regarded as deeply offensive and immoral. Indeed rape is generally regarded as a far greater sin than adultery, for it denies the woman in question her autonomy, that is, her possession of her own body.

When we turn to same-sex relationships, the difficulties of the historical task multiply. In our society, we are used to the concepts of the 'homosexual' and 'sexual orientation'; that is we are acquainted with the idea that persons are understood to have an identity in which their erotic preference is to the fore. It is *'their* sexuality', that is, it is autonomous and in some sense defines who they are. We therefore tend to assume that individuals with a sense of identity as persons conscious of being different, of being erotically attracted to members of their own sex, existed well before the word 'homosexual' (coined in 1869 by the Hungarian writer Karl Maria Kertbeny as part of a burgeoning medical and scientific vocabulary) came to identify them as such. Indeed much of the current debate assumes that the existence of such a personal identity has remained a stable and unchanging fact of sexual life throughout the ages. Hence the frequent parallels drawn with race and the argument that the contemporary emancipation of gay people is analogous to the historical abolition of slavery.

Yet there is no real evidence for such an identity prior to the seventeenth century, and even into the eighteenth century most men 'who committed sodomy did not think of themselves other than as ordinary, everyday members of society. They did not belong to a subculture, nor did they have a distinctive self-identity' (Hitchcock, 1997, p. 63). While we might understand and categorize their behaviour as homosexual in character, their contemporaries appear to have seen such activity as an extension of the forms of sexual behaviour common to courting and marriage. Indeed, our contemporary western way of thinking is far from common, for even in societies where homosexual acts are publicly accepted, even regarded as normative, they are certainly not seen as the most salient or significant factor about the person who engages in them, even when they are expressed exclusively between people of the same sex. Thus, while there have almost certainly been people exclusively attracted to members of the same sex across all human cultures and throughout history, it is only in the eighteenth century or so that such individuals begin to be defined, by themselves and others, as different, that is, as persons with an identity which possesses a distinctive cultural and, in time, historical consciousness.

Indeed it is this distinctive development that underpins some of the fraught character of the debate between Anglicans. For, when they talk about sexual acts between persons of the same sex, different parts of the Anglican Communion are, quite literally, addressing different cultural categories, and lack of recognition of this exacerbates theological and other differences between them.

If we are to truly understand the past, we need then to unthink this central category and prepare ourselves for the unexpected as we turn back the clock and consider how gay identity arose and how it might relate (if at all) to the words and concepts that had previously been applied to those engaging in sexual acts with members of the same sex, most obviously the 'abominable sodomite'.

## Intimate friendship in early modern England

We live in a conjugal age, that is, in a culture in which the most significant intimate relationships are those between couples. The contemporary ideal is that such relationships are marked by equality between the partners, a commitment to permanence, mutual reciprocity, self-sacrifice and a high level of emotional interdependence. And indeed, we may lament or blame the rise of individualism or 'selfishness' for corroding and compromising this ideal. Other commitments, beyond the immediate family, be they to kin, friends or the wider community, are understood to be second order.

For our predecessors in early modern England, that is, in the sixteenth and seventeenth centuries, things were very different indeed. First, society was profoundly patriarchal and the political, moral and economic authority of the head of the household over all its members including his wife was a powerful reality. Second, marriage was not simply located within a more influential kinship group in which relatives, especially those who were older and of higher status, had greater influence and authority over individuals, but rather within a much broader and more 'untidy' set of relationships in which friendship played a central role. On a day-to-day basis, the composition of households was complex, with servants (some of whom might have been the children of poorer relatives), apprentices, lodgers and business partners, in addition to the 'nuclear' family, all living together. The spaces and activities that went to make up intimate living including the sharing of beds was primarily homosocial, that is, between members of the same sex, as indeed were the main bonds of affection. Furthermore, many men, including some who were married, were attached to great houses or places of education and lived almost exclusively with other men. For two men to share a bed, engage in strong expressions of physical affection like kissing, caress-ing and hugging, or within certain social strata to write letters express-ing their love and affection using language we would expect of lovers, was not only unremarkable, it was central to the fabric of society.

Thus to the modern mind, to read of one man's recollection of a time when 'the bed's head could not be found between the Master and his dog [i.e. himself]' (Bray 2003, p. 154) is to conjure immediately the suspicion that a sexual relationship might exist between the two – in this case between the author of the epistle, the Duke of Buckingham, and his king, James I. Yet, we need to be extremely careful in drawing such conclusions from writings with strong homoerotic tones, even in relation to a man, like James, who had a succession of young men as his 'favourites'. For despite their intimacies, such 'familiar' letters did not belong entirely to the realm of the private, indeed they were often intended to be read by others as statements of public, and in that sense political, obligation and commitment between friends and allies. And to be the bedfellow of the king was in effect a political position – to be the monarch's gatekeeper and confidant.

This 'lost world' of intense and close male friendships was also a world deeply informed and influenced by ideas of intimate friendship drawn from the biblical examples of David and Jonathan and of the Beloved Disciple and our Lord. Caution should thus be exercised in our evalu-ation of the relationship between James and Buckingham: it may have had a sexual dimension in the sense of genital contact, or it may not have done; we simply do not have the evidence to make such a judge-ment should we so wish. Likewise, it is speculative to assert that the biblical record implies that David's love of Jonathan, 'surpassing the love of women', involved sexual activity.

It is however quite clear that same-sex friendships in medieval and early modern England involved a degree of commitment and affection that surpasses our contemporary expectations. But there is more. We have very clear evidence of relationships between men, and less often between women, that are described in quasi-marital terms and involved profound mutual commitment, sacrifice and affection. Furthermore, such relationships were publicly and ritually formalized in Christian cere-monies, characteristically in celebrations of Holy Communion (Bray 2003). Historians have been aware of the existence of same-sex ceremonies or 'sworn brotherhood' for a number of years, not least as a result of the publication of *The Marriage of Likeness* in 1994 by John Boswell. Boswell argued that such ceremonies demonstrated a public affirmation of relation-ships that involved sexual intimacy. However, more recent and detailed scholarship is much more cautious, tantalizingly neither confirming nor denying that possibility. But it does provide clear evidence of profound mutual commitment through a different sort of shared bed: the grave. For, rather poignantly, gravestones and monuments erected to such committed friends can be discovered over a remarkably long historical period, from that to be found in Istanbul for the crusading knights Sir William Neville and Sir John Clanvowe, who died together in 1371, and whose two helmets meet in stone as if kissing on their monument, to the simple grave Cardinal John Newman shared with his friend Ambrose St John, who predeceased him by 14 years in 1875.

In so far as history can be persuaded to give up her secrets, it is simply incontestable that many of these relationships were marked by love, support, mutual understanding and a range of the sort of reciprocities, both long and short term, which we would be gratified to see within a modern marriage. Indeed in many ways such same-sex friendships, being more equal in character, might be deemed much closer to our contemporary ideal of marriage than the more hierarchal unions of the sixteenth century, burdened as they were with the concerns of household, property transmission and indeed the reproduction of society.

So did such people in ritually established same-sex relationships give of themselves sexually to each other? Again, we must be cautious, for it is unlikely that our categories and distinctions will map onto historical understandings. It also seems a little prurient to enquire, and for the most part we simply don't have the evidence. There is, however, one very clear and explicit exception to this, and it is exceptional in two regards – it is very late, coming in the early nineteenth century and it involves a relationship between two women, Anne Lister, a Yorkshire heiress of considerable means, and Ann Walker. Nevertheless it is clear from Lister's extensive diaries (in 27 volumes) and from contemporary accounts that her union with Ann Walker stands within this long tradition, being a public relationship involving the exchange of rings and solemnization in church on Easter Day in 1834. The diaries also recount details of their shared sexual intimacy.

Despite the uncertainty and indeed the ambiguity which in the main attends these sworn friendships, we can be quite sure that whatever did or did not occur, such individuals were not 'sodomites'.

## The sodomite and the 'unnatural order'

'Sodomy' was a criminal offence in England and Wales from 1562 onwards, punishable by hanging. It was considered the sin above all sins. In terms of the law however there was a great deal of ambiguity with its definition, for sodomy seems to have covered anal penetration of a man or woman, bestiality, the molestation of children and, at least in theory, sexual acts between women. In practice however the overwhelming majority of those few who were successfully prosecuted seem to have been guilty of some sort of sexual assault and more lenient punishments were handed down to those few convicted of consensual sexual acts. Indeed careful historical analysis seems to suggest that tolerance of consensual 'deviant' sexual behaviour was much higher than its status as a capital offence would suggest, and that when it occurred it wasn't 'recognized' as sodomy. A sort of doublethink operated: those who participated in sexual acts with a person of the same sex were patently not sodomites for they did not fit the clear profile of a sodomite, therefore they could not be committing sodomy. How then can we understand such a contradiction?

All human communities have a need to affirm the identity and indeed the boundaries of their group; to reimagine and reaffirm the values that bind it together and distinguish it as a moral community separate from other human groups. This results in the creation and elaboration of what we might describe as a symbolic world-view, an imaginative construction that is often at some distance from observed reality. Such a world-view seeks to maintain coherence and identity in the face of threat. It seeks order, meaning and coherence in the face of a life that is in constant flux, where things do not run to plan, misfortune abounds and plans are dashed. Collective shared anxieties and fears are thus frequently placed upon various 'outsiders' or 'aliens' who are then negatively construed: for example 'Commies', Jews, Catholics, 'niggers', or 'sponging' asylum-seekers. All of these are symbolic constructions; that is, they are identities, groups of people hated primarily as imagined invisible abstractions with stereotypical characteristics, rather than in the more concrete form of Patrick or Errol or Maria who lives next door and may not in fact be recognized as a member of the labelled group, despite their politics or ethnicity, for their known humanity doesn't 'fit'. The fact that we are dealing here with abstractions is brought home to us by the observation that in certain times and places those with a real reference are mixed in with fantastical identities. Perhaps the most obvious and compelling example of such an irrational abstraction is the witch.

Another is the sodomite. For in the early modern period, we find that the category of the 'sodomite' in Renaissance England closely linked in public rhetoric with the world of witches, werewolves and basilisks (see Bray 1996). It is even more closely associated in early Protestant England with the pope and his treacherous, heretical disciples. Hence the visceral language of sexuality is used to reinforce the boundaries of the social order of Elizabethan England and beyond, deployed against their traditional political and religious enemies, lurking across the Channel in Catholic Europe.

Furthermore, just as everyone 'knew' what a typical witch looked like and how she acted, so too everyone knew that a sodomite was a libertine distinguished by his extreme debauchery. He was an identifiable type with a pretty young man on one arm and his whore or mistress on the other, a byword then for an excessive and coercive carnality that knew no bounds.

The sodomite of the Renaissance imagination therefore simultaneously conjured the degraded nature of the political and religious threat to social order and provided an extreme example of the indiscriminate depths to which a human could fall. It was a warning to all that sodomy was potentially universal, that men (and conceivably) women were at heart, as the Marriage Service of the Book of Common Prayer puts it, 'brute beasts that have no understanding'. Such a conception – that if social and moral rules were relaxed, 'homosexual acts', like other sins, could break out indiscriminately – is of course radically at odds with the contemporary ideal of same-sex Christian friendship. So it is with our contemporary psychosocial understanding of the gay man or lesbian as a person who has an exclusive or predominant sexual attraction, who is, as we say, *oriented* towards another person of the same sex.

Nevertheless, the potency of such 'symbolic' language continues to be evoked and used to reaffirm the central values of traditionally minded communities. Fears that once the rules are 'relaxed' chaos could ensue find extensive echoes in much contemporary Christian thinking about sexuality; in discussions about the curricula for sex education in schools; and, indeed in the argument that the 'sanctity of marriage' is best protected by blanket prohibitions on the expression of homosexuality. That heterosexual marriage is somehow protected by prohibitions which would increase the possibility of those with same-sex erotic attraction being 'trapped' unhappily within traditional marriages fails the test of reason, yet the endorsement of such a position serves very effectively to unite the community of those who advocate and reaffirm traditional values against what they fear might be the dilution of the faith by other believers.

## Things are a-changing

Witches and basilisks are a thing of the past, but so too is the ideal and the associated practices of Christian friendship characteristic of the sixteenth and seventeenth centuries. For from the mid-seventeenth century onwards, a number of social changes were initiated that have continued to the present day, not least those associated with the rapidly evolving nation state which brought about a shift in the balance of people's obligations and loyalties, away from extended kin, local patrons and the local community, towards other emergent institutions and a growing sense of national citizenship. As a result there was a fresh emphasis on individual autonomy, a strengthening of what we have come to call the 'nuclear family' and greater emphasis on the bond between husband and wife. Selection of a partner was less influenced by the wider family group and its economic interests, and more by the personal desires of the couple themselves (Stone 1977). From this period onwards it was, increasingly, wives and husbands, rather than other same-sex friends, who were one's closest companions (literally, 'those with whom one breaks bread'), those with whom one shared the intimate and every-day moments of living together, who could be relied upon and to whom one was morally obliged. As a result, as the eighteenth century progressed both women and children gained much greater autonomy and the home became a more markedly private world. This shift had a number of major consequences and gave birth to one rather surprising social innovation.

## 'Molly' houses

The so-called 'molly' houses seem to have emerged in the late-seventeenth century. Remarkably prevalent, especially in London, molly houses were for the most part taverns or ale houses, though some seemed to have been private houses, where men met to socialize, gossip, flirt and drink. They were also places where men had sex with each other away from the gaze of the law. Perhaps more significantly, the molly houses created a very distinctive subculture based on ironic elaborations and inversions of heterosexual interaction; with dress codes, language and rituals being marked by an extravagant effeminacy and cross-dressing. Although only visitors, regular or infrequent, to such establishments, members (or 'mollies') could not fail to see themselves at some level as people who were different. Here, those whose affections and perhaps sexual relationships could no longer be concealed within the homosocial world of bedfellows, whose homoerotic desires could find shelter no more under the codes of Christian friendship, found a place to be – crucially with others who were similarly inclined. Not, of course, that it went unopposed. In particular, the eighteenth century witnessed a series of raids and high-profile trials, the result of the zealous activities of the Societies for the Reformation of Manners, whose agents sought to root out such vice and bring prosecutions. Yet, despite such harassment, the molly houses continued to exist, apparently tolerated, albeit grudgingly, by neighbours for decades. Indeed it is to such institutions that modern gay culture owes its early origins.

The increasing centrality of the role of affection between husband and wife also contributed to a development central to how we have come to understand the meaning of sexual intimacy between people, namely family limitation.

## Family limitation and the changing character of marriage

The preface of the modern marriage service speaks of the gift that is marriage bringing husband and wife together 'in the delight and tenderness of sexual union'. However, for most of the Christian period, there have been quite severe limits on the degree to which sex could be experienced as pleasurable between men and women, for it has a weighty consequence: pregnancy. Furthermore, the fundamental justification for sex was held to be procreation, and indeed the creation of the next generation was a central concern for individuals, families and larger social groups, especially in the context of high and fluctuating levels of mortality. Prior to the late nineteenth century in Europe, to be a married woman was to be engaged in a relentless cycle of gestation, breastfeeding and childcare.

However, in the nineteenth century, infant and child mortality began to fall significantly and irreversibly, bringing about a substantial population increase in many European countries and, at the level of the individual household, a greater expectation that most children would make it into adulthood. Such a situation, aided by the first stirrings of female emancipation, increased medical understanding, and the advocacy of family limitation led many late Victorians to the acceptance of it, either out of a desire to 'spare' their wives the still high risk of morbidity and mortality (for soldiers aside, few men ever ran the 'occupational health' risks that equate to giving birth in the absence of modern standards of health and hygiene!) or to lessen the potential economic burden of large families, given the higher survival rates. Such family limitation was initially achieved by *coitus interruptus* and abstinence, but during the early decades of the twentieth century artificial contraceptives were increasingly used. Medical and ecclesiastical authorities vehemently opposed such methods at first, but as awareness dawned of the radical nature of change brought about by the fall in death rates, there was a clear need for ethical reassessment. At its meeting in 1930, the Lambeth Conference (Resolution 15) grudgingly approved family limitation, 'where there is clearly felt moral obligation to limit or avoid parenthood'. By 1958 the new situation was embraced more fully, as Resolution 115 makes clear:

The Conference believes that the responsibility for deciding upon the number and frequency of children has been laid by God upon the consciences of parents everywhere; that this planning, in such ways as are mutually acceptable to husband and wife in Christian conscience, is a right and important factor in Christian family life and should be the result of positive choice before God. Such responsible parenthood, built on obedience to all the duties of marriage, requires a wise stewardship of the resources and abilities of the family as well as a thoughtful consideration of the varying population needs and problems of society and the claims of future generations.

Written into this affirmation is an awareness that the use of contraception might be a prudent and positive moral choice in light of the limited resources within the family and indeed, at a much larger scale, human populations. Yet this ethical reassessment constitutes a radical development within the Christian tradition. For from the second century onwards, the weight of tradition, from Augustine to Aquinas and beyond, and indeed the contemporary Roman Catholic Church, has been clear that the procreation of children is central to the understanding of marriage and the role of sexuality within it. This twentieth-century discernment accompanied by a greater appreciation of the role of sexuality in strengthening the union of the couples' hearts and lives has led to a clear understanding that within a permanent, faithful and exclusive relationship, non-reproductive sexuality was not just valid, but a blessing. While such a shift stands in stark contrast with the weight of Christian tradition, it receives strong scriptural support from a number of key texts including the early chapters of Genesis, the Song of Songs and Hosea, where the theological emphasis in marriage is placed on the relationship between the man and the woman rather than upon the fruits of their activities. As such it has led to an entirely appropriate re-evaluation of the character and role of sexual desire and its relationship to our call to be persons responding to the call of Christ.

## Concluding reflections

It might be thought, and indeed argued, that the content of sexual ethics, unlike say medical ethics, is fixed, for new ethical dilemmas are posed by the advances of science and technology, but our bodies and our desires remain constant. Yet, integral to our understanding of personhood is the idea and the reality that we are constituted in large part by our relationships with others – with God, with parents, with our brothers and sisters in Christ. We are deeply social in our make-up and thus our desires and actions are only fully comprehensible when that broader context is understood. Sexual ethics will then inevitably undergo some development or refinement over time as a result of significant social change. One of the most profound changes in the post-Reformation period has been a shift in authority within the family from a patriarchal to a more egalitarian model. This has entailed a radical shift within Christianity of the nature and status of women. The consequences of this have been far-reaching and indeed are still unfolding (for example, in the consideration of female episcopacy in the Church of England). One of these consequences has been the development of a more equal and emotionally intense relationship within marriage, admittedly perhaps to the detriment of other relationships. Another has been the emergence of gay identity and the desire, on the part of some Christian believers, to enter a loving and intimate relationship with the same discipline as traditional marriage, that is, that it be faithful, exclusive and permanent.

Like Anglicans of just two or three generations ago wrestling with the issue of whether contraception was permissible, we find ourselves, in considering same-sex relationships, entering into new territory. While we cannot pretend this is anything other than a new place, the historical existence of committed, affectionate, publicly sanctioned and *at some level* intimate relationships should give us significant food for thought.

The positive and prudent use of contraception within marriage has deepened our understanding of the contribution that sexual desire and activity make to the deepening union of hearts and minds between persons so committed. It entailed a radical, yet quite proper ethical reassessment of the tradition by church leaders and theologians. However, this profound change was pioneered by faithful lay women and men reflecting on their everyday experience and responsibilities as men and women, as parents and as Christians. In seeking then to discern God's will for our brothers and sisters in Christ who are gay, we must pay close attention to the central role of experience.

# References

Boswell, J., *The Marriage of Likeness*, HarperCollins, London, 1994.

Bray, A., *The Friend*, University of Chicago Press, Chicago, 2003.

Bray, A., *Homosexuality in Renaissance England*, Columbia University Press, Colombia, 1996.

Hartley, L. P., *The Go-Between*, Hamish Hamilton, London, 1953.

Hitchcock, T., *English Sexualities 1700–1800*, Macmillan, London, 1997.

Stone, L., *Family, Sex and Marriage in England 1500–1800*, Harper & Row, London, 1977.

# Part 3

# REASON AND PERSONHOOD

Being made in the image of God, we have no alternative but to exercise our reason and reflect upon experience in the light of Christ's call upon our lives. Paying close attention to the past and to the experiences of historical Christians can bring challenge to our theological categories and ideas. Similarly, advances in scientific and other forms of knowledge and the test of whether something rings 'true to our experience' can disturb, challenge and cast light on the truths concerning our bodily existence and sexuality.

In her essay Jessica Martin draws attention to the dangers of a 'thoughtless and clumsy application of the rules' by bringing us back to the person of Christ. While allowing that they have their proper place, she argues that we often hide behind rules to avoid Christ's 'greater' demands. This is particularly true in the arena of our bodily existence. As she points out, 'It is a terrifying challenge, to live in the body.'

That challenge is especially tortuous for those whose bodies do not conform to 'normal' expectations as John Hare demonstrates in his chapter on intersexuality, which considers those men and women whose bodies are neither clearly male nor female. In his discussion of the various conditions that go to make up intersexuality, and their medical management, he raises some fundamental questions about our theological understanding of the nature of the difference between the sexes and its implications, with clear consequences for the debate about same-sex relationships.

Finally, Arnold Browne explores some of the ways in which attitudes to sexual desire and sexual activity have been inextricably linked to ideas about race, gender and status. While persistent throughout human history and culture and supported, sometimes zealously, by Christian preachers and writers, many of these connections – like the prohibition on interracial marriage – are profoundly at odds with contemporary Christian understandings of the gospel. Yet it is these historical and cultural understandings that have shaped much of the traditional opposition to the expression of sexuality between members of the same sex.

# 7

# Thinking about Christ's body; thinking about his face

JESSICA MARTIN

The physicality of Christ is a thing most wonderful, almost too wonderful to be. His particular body, born, growing to maturity, living in historical time, killed by fellow humans and gloriously resurrected, founds the Church. When we too, who make up his Church, are called his Body, we are reminded again of his physicality and of our own: our hands, the Church's instruments, are called to act for Christ in the physical world.

Bodiliness is then the sacred heart of Christianity. Christ himself stands as the shining difference between Christianity and the other great monotheisms — not that we have a code, or have formulated an ethic of living in a particular way. The wonder of the incarnation certainly makes extraordinary demands upon all of us who work to live in Christ; but codes of life, in the sense that they are understood by Judaism or by Islam, are not at the heart of those demands.

It is true that Christians often talk as if they were. Yet when we do so we are like a married woman on the verge of rebellion and therefore only able to articulate the shape of her marriage in terms of the vows she took. Such a perspective hovers on the border between faithfulness and betrayal, because it contemplates the edges of a relationship and ignores its centre. The face of our beloved is not in the fact of our vows. Codes do many things: they may be socially necessary; they belong to the Church as to every other human institution; but they do not describe or narrate lives. Sometimes, without regard for the human face, they proscribe them.

In Christ, the Body is sacred. This means that the human body is a sacred space, in all its aspects, however mundane: living the Christian life is a sacred act. The New Testament is rich with this knowledge. The story of Jesus' life is full of moments when touch transforms. His saliva restores a man's sight (Mark 8.22–26; John 9.1–12); he weeps in the face of a friend's death (John 11.1–44); a woman who touches his clothes in a crowd is healed of a 12-year haemorrhage (Matthew 9.20–23;

Mark 5.25–34; Luke 8.43–48). Judas' kiss ratifies the enormity of his betrayal, prefigured in their sharing food in the same dish (Matthew 26.14–50; Mark 14.10–46; Luke 22.1–48; John 13.1–30). Members of the early Church, understanding themselves to be part of Christ's Body, find equally rich, interlocking metaphors to illuminate that understanding. They are 'living stones' (1 Peter 2.5) – a sacred building made of breathing, acting bodies; they are each a 'temple of the Holy Spirit' (1 Corinthians 6.19; 2 Corinthians 6.16) – a breathing, acting body which is also a sacred building. We are, and do, holiness.

## Holiness and sexuality

Our human bodiliness is interwoven with our sexuality: they are not separable. Throughout Christian history people have coped with this fact in different ways. In the early years of the Church the dangers and complexities of sexuality were so clearly recognized that for many the only answer seemed to lie in extreme physical discipline – not only in celibacy, but in asceticism, the denying of the body food, sleep, adequate covering, shelter. The most thoughtful practitioners of asceticism recognized that these activities were themselves responses to bodiliness, and came to terms with that realization; many others hoped (vainly) to lose the body altogether in pursuing purely spiritual fulfilment. In doing so Christianity's distinctive immediacy was lost to them; nor did asceticism silence the demands of the body. Rather it amplified them. Extreme asceticism no longer seems to most modern Christians a useful route towards holiness, although sensible bodily disciplines helpfully inform many devotional routines. We are stuck (to put it negatively) with our bodies and the demands they make; sexuality is interwoven into all those demands.

Therefore, most urgently, we need to find a way in which our sexuality may be part of the holiness we work to inhabit. I don't just mean in the expression of the sexual act. That is simply at the most unambiguous end of our sexualized interactions. Our sexuality affects all our relationships and needs always to be managed attentively; we are creatures on a continuum; we are not polarized. A father's relationships with the female friends of his teenage daughter, for example, will have to find a way to negotiate the attractions of youth and burgeoning sexuality. Whatever he chooses (let's say he manages it by making lots of joky references to his own decrepitude) will fall into an awkward category between flirting and fatherliness. But he probably won't be planning to sleep with them. Rules only take you so far – they only tell you about boundaries and borders; they safeguard the centre, but are fundamentally uninterested as to what the centre really is.

This means that the more ambiguous level on which our sexuality operates seldom has straightforward prohibitions or codes attached. We can sin within the rules. Someone can, for example, truly claim they have remained 'faithful' to their spouse, or to their vows of celibacy, while entering on a separate and very intimate relationship with a friend which either involves no physical contact or physical contact defined as 'neutral'. Perhaps they are largely right. Only they, and perhaps the friend, know how far that relationship is driven by sexual feeling. We recognize some forms of unfaithfulness (flirting, for example) though our judgement on it tends to be gentle. Other failures of trust we have no technical names for. Christ's words in Matthew, 'every one who looks at a woman lustfully has already committed adultery with her in his heart' (5.28), recognize that these failures of trust exist and are bound to exist. The context of what he says, though, suggests that this rigorous attentiveness to our own feelings and motives is not meant to be punitive, but the opposite; in recognizing our own mistakes, we have compassion on the mistakes of others.

This too is a negative view: that is to say, it focuses upon our sexual failings rather than upon the richness and the potential of human sexual complexity. Perhaps this is because this richness is by its nature not easy to spot in the records of human history; perhaps also because it is not made manifest by even the most complex of moral codes. The disasters we can cause through sexual expression, on the other hand, tend to make themselves obvious. But not all kinds of prayerful attentiveness to our sexual responses are about having compassion on mistakes. It is likely that the majority are focused quite differently. Whether we are prepared to recognize it or not, there will be some sexualized element, however muted or transmuted, in our ordinary interactions with both sexes, and we will have ways of living with that. Not all – indeed not many – of those ways will be horrified or penitential, unless we are on very bad terms indeed with our own flesh; a great number will recognize and celebrate the energy released into our purposes and friendships by this route. In a less public context close friendships, held as they are in a sensitive rapport with another person, flourish harmoniously within mutual boundaries; and it may not be at all visible to those on the outside where those boundaries lie. It may not even be relevant for outsiders. The *meanings* of bodily decorum are known only to God.

This is not a weaselly way of saying anything goes. Rules may not be adequate for people but they are certainly necessary. Yet it is also true that rules change. They change gradually in response to a collective discernment about human need and human dignity, which is the work of the Spirit in the Body of Christ. I'll take an extreme example: Christians do not believe that the Lord requires us to stone a man to death for gathering firewood on the sabbath (Numbers 15.32–36). Rather we believe that the sabbath should be honoured. So, because these two things – that rules are necessary but that they are not adequate – are held in tension for us, we need to give prohibitions very considerable respect and attention, more attention than can be expressed through their thoughtless and clumsy application. They are the boundaries of the sacredness of our trust: to embody the love of Christ, to conform our own bodies to express that love. We need to submit all interactions to that discipline. The truth is that Jesus imposes *greater* demands upon us with respect to our physical behaviour than can be encoded within the boundaries of law.

Look at his attitude to fasting (Matthew 6.16–18). When he places more value on concealed fasting than on its open, formal observance he moves the category of the worthy fast from a piece of fairly automatic public behaviour to an emotionally costly, private expression of sorrow-with-consequences. The former is a lot easier than the latter. Recognizing this, Jesus also offers us the grace and wisdom of the Holy Spirit to help us live out his demands. Rules will not disentangle the complexities of our reactions to each other. We will not learn that haemorrhaging women are pure members of the kingdom by scrutinizing biblical prohibitions, but by looking at Jesus' actions.

Sexual behaviour is not neutral. Christians can't say, as much of modern secular society does, that what happens between consenting adults is somehow on one side of behavioural ethics, of habits of living; or that it's all OK 'if no one's hurt'. How is that guaranteed, anyway, when sexuality is so bound up with human vulnerability? How may we discern how to proceed in so complex and tricky an area? What guidance do we have? Hurting and being hurt are after all part of the risk of every relationship, however peripherally related to the sexual. How do we learn to 'live in love'? It is a terrifying challenge, to live in the body.

The enormity of the demands of incarnational living is, therefore, a part – a large part – of why Christians find the sexuality issue so urgent and so painful. On top of this no Christian can say that sexuality is morally neutral unless they make a stupidly artificial distinction between bodiliness and sexuality. How then do we present our bodies a living sacrifice; in what way do we conform our sexuality to a life in Christ? It's not a solution simply to confine the issue to performing, or avoiding performing, explicit sexual acts; it is a complex picture, not the simple 'do it like this and with this person and God says you'll be OK' model currently favoured by some prominent voices in the debate.

## Same-sex desire

For the many Christians whose primary sexual response is to another person of the same sex the question has a particular and appalling urgency. The burden of it is one that the sexuality debate within the Church has done nothing to lessen. If every sexualized response, however subtle, becomes a matter for moral care (as I argue here that it should) then for every Christian homosexual person, as things stand at present, life becomes quickly unendurable. If on the other hand it is only about who does what with whom in bed then all of us are off the hook with respect to a multitude of important connections and betrayals. Think of Bill Clinton defending the terms of his relationship with Monica Lewinski with the downright assertion, 'I did not have sexual relations with that woman.' According to one (non-penetrative) understanding of what the sexual act consists in, he was precise rather than false. It is all just a matter of where you draw the line.

However, even then, for the homosexual the line is drawn in a different place. For the heterosexual there are situations in which explicit sexual acts are not forbidden; for the homosexual there are not. Although by keeping to the letter of this definitional law, you could, if homosexual, allow yourself some limited sexual expression, you could never allow yourself – or your partner – any intimacy *defined* as sexual. (Different people would, no doubt, define things differently in any case. Fewer people thought Clinton truthful than he hoped.) The Christian homosexual is therefore forced into a life where there is no explicit place for sexual desire – except anywhere not claimed as a place for sexual desire. This is potentially a frightening state of affairs, likely to cause a warped and terrible relationship between the self and the body, not to mention warped and terrible relationships between bodies. It is not incarnational, requiring, as it does, a good deal of self-deceit to carry off. It is quite different from a call to celibacy and is not a good reason to choose the celibate life. Celibacy is, or should be, independent of the sexual orientation of the person called. It is about an offering of the self to God by serving his creatures, never making an exclusive choice of a particular partner. Celibates learn the discipline of bodily love differently and more publicly. It is not a route that can be safely traversed by refusing to consider matters of desire (Nouwen 2001).

It seems, then, that the choice at present, if you have a same-sex orientation, is between evils. You might allow yourself most of the gamut of ambiguous sexual responses while never expecting any complete sexual fulfilment for you or for anyone you might love in that way. You would of course never let yourself think about the misleading messages you might be giving out. Alternatively you could spend your energy on rigorously suppressing every sexualized response for fear of influencing someone, anyone at all, in your direction. Your motives would not be the call to celibacy but a fear of your own self: not the perfect love which casts out fear but an act of that violence – directed against the self – which fear breeds. One option mostly hurts others; the other mostly hurts yourself.

It is, of course, not always right to choose to express a sexual response. The act of expressing what should have been left latent can corrupt a relationship and hurt those involved. Self-control is central to human behaviour and to our regard for our neighbour. However, opponents of homosexuality would define any part of its expression as corrupting. This is a very sweeping definition indeed, requiring homosexuality itself to be an evil and its clear presence in human sexual activity to be part of the fallenness of the world. In such a vision, same-sex desire is a horror more recently characterized quasi-medically as a pathology, or even as a disability. It becomes a quirk in the way God made some humans akin to the physical mis-makings of disease, and like those physical mis-makings, something that impedes the full expression of human joy and possibility that God intends for his creatures.

This point about the definition of homosexuality as something *medically* awry (which sounds so much more scientific and unarguable with than a reaction based on disgust or even on moral judgement) is particularly important. We inherit a history in which serious violence has been done to the lives of men and women defined as 'suffering' from the pathology which is homosexuality. The first section of *Some Issues of Human Sexuality* (House of Bishops Group 2003) gives a summary of part – largely the legislative part – of this history; John Hare, in this volume, tells us more about its medical antecedents and the ambiguousness of the physiology of gender. If homosexuality is not a pathology, then defining it as one is a very great injustice. The burden of proof lies with those who claim it to be one, because the case is not self-evident. The existence of even one same-sex relationship rooted in faithful and generous love calls it most seriously into question. Even one such relationship makes manifest that very flowering of human joy and possibility that the fact of homosexuality was supposed to impede. There are many such relationships: that is simply a matter of fact.

Homosexual relationships, like heterosexual relationships, have the potential for exploitation and cruelty; but not in the fact of both partners being of the same gender. Indeed one might expect homosexual partnerships to be free of many of the embedded cruelties of heterosexual partnerships, the ways in which they imitate and express worldly power and domination through marriages of convenience, or the way that throughout much of history and in many parts of the world women have been bred up to the service of men, kept ignorant and without choices and married off young in order to serve masculine needs and ambitions. Or – to take a different tack – are homosexual relationships to be pathologized because they do not produce children, in which case should all childless couples be thought of in the same way? Once upon a time barren marriages were crippled ones. To think that now would be a kind of obscenity.

When we pay due attention to our sexual responses, from the most ambiguous to the most clear, we have to acknowledge that they exist with respect to all the human beings we encounter, although they will be likely (though not certain) to be stronger for one gender than for the other. Absolute heterosexuality, then, is also a construct, once we are thinking sensitively about our interactions with each other. Another way of putting this is to say that the spectrum of human sexual response given to us is more broad, beautiful and subtle than we formerly realized. The glaring primary colours which belong to a view of sexuality defined only by reproduction – and thus an aggressively heterosexual view – destroy or bleach out shades associated with subtle feeling altogether; we cannot simply apply them now we know that sexual feeling drives so much of who and what we are. We have to express our Christian sexual ethic in some other way.

## Recognizing others

Embodied Christianity requires us to make acts of *recognition*. That is to say, as Christ recognized those he touched and healed, so we are required to recognize each other. When we recognize someone we notice their otherness, their difference from us, at the same time as we celebrate the connection between us. Our sympathy identifies them – it may even mean that we identify *with* them – but we don't appropriate who they are or decide they are 'just like us'. We notice that they are not us.

When our acts of true recognition are also sexual encounters then they move riskily beyond this point, to a place where one self opens to the other; a rare gift, and in a fallen world a dangerous one. For its very riskiness makes it a fitting image for joyful surrender in the presence of God: as in the devotional use of the Song of Songs, or in the picture of Christ as his Church's Bridegroom. At its very best, a precious shadow of this is available in sexual love: in the closing verses of Ephesians 5 this absolute bodily self-giving is described as a 'great mystery'. We may see through a glass, and darkly, but what we see is the hazy outline of our Beloved's face.

Of course, much sexual encounter is really not very like this at all, whether in faithful monogamous relationships or not. We are mundane as well as ecstatic in our bodily living – in sex too. We can model faithfulness in living without constant ecstasy of self-giving, just as relationships with God are also at times dry, or matters of habit. Our encounters with God and each other are ordinary as well as extraordinary. But a habit of recognition allows us to negotiate those encounters and to be sensitive to a decorum about the rareness of self-giving, which when it comes is not always sexual (it might happen, for example, in those moments of intimacy in a family around a bereavement). Mutuality can never be imposed. But because sexual response is so powerful we need to recognize that the vulnerability it requires means faithfulness and commitment are vital safeguards. The briefest of explicit sexual encounters imposes an intimacy like no other.

## Discernment in debate

There are a few other things we need to bear in mind as we struggle to live our lives of embodied recognition. Christianity as it operates in the world is a secular institution as well as a sacred mode of life, in a fallen universe operating between Pentecost and the *Parousia*, Christ's coming again. Therefore it has its own codes, its politics, its hierarchies and its power struggles, all of which are bound up with the demands of the world. Do certain codes, however derived, dehumanize for reasons other than the demands of a God of love? We need to be intelligent about discerning when the pressures of power are leading a debate of this kind. I am not alone in believing that there are other, more politicized reasons why the homosexuality debate is currently so very vexed and so very public.

Yet there is always a spark of the Spirit's life inside the constricting shell of Christian politics and administration, pushing against some of its demands when they in their turn push human beings and human potentialities out of shape. Throughout the Bible many of its writers express a profound tension between codes of living and the life of God: it is full of unexpected and undeserved acts of mercy, gifts 'without money and without price' (Isaiah 55.1). Therefore we need to be attentive to our own codes, even if they are problematically articulated in those sacred books; do we know that they are any more reliable than the Jewish code which found a menstruating woman unclean?

We need more humility, more attentiveness to each other, even if such attention makes us all alarmingly vulnerable. We need to listen to what God is telling us, instead of shouting at each other. More fundamentally even than this, we need more humility in the face of the complexity of God's creation. Though we are at present embattled, hurling certainties as weapons from opposite corners, we are in essence and at our best united in a genuine attempt to discern how to embody Christian living in our collective understanding of sexuality. May we find ways to recognize each other, to celebrate the diversity of the human face within the Body of Christ.

# References

House of Bishops Group, *Some Issues in Human Sexuality: A Guide to the Debate*, Church House Publishing, London, 2003.

Nouwen, H., *Clowning in Rome: Reflections on Solitude, Celibacy, Prayer*, Darton, Longman & Todd, London, 2001.

# 8

# 'Neither male nor female': the case of intersexuality

## JOHN HARE

On 11 March 2006 the *Guardian* carried an article by a young woman, Helen Scully, about the effects of what she called her 'wonky gene'. Helen has Androgen Insufficiency Syndrome (AIS), a condition that prevents the development of her uterus and fallopian tubes and has left her with a shortened vagina, which she has had to enlarge to make sexual intercourse possible. Furthermore, her gonads have had to be removed because of the significant risk that they will become cancerous. She sums up her painful struggle in the following words: 'Being AIS is about more than having a wonky gene, it's about struggling to be who you are in a world that can be at odds with you.'

Helen is by conventional criteria male because she possesses a Y chromosome and her chromosomal make-up is therefore that for a normal male (46XY). The underdeveloped gonads were testes, not ovaries. However, as a result of AIS, she was unable to respond to the male hormones produced in the weeks after conception and develop as a male. She has developed instead into what may be described, biologically, as the fallback position: externally she is an undeveloped female but internally her development has been so arrested that she is neither clearly male nor female.

People like Helen are members of a group who are best described as intersexual. This group is composed of individuals with a range of medical conditions but all members have one factor in common: that for each one, when all the usual determinants of maleness and femaleness are put together, that person cannot be clearly assigned to a male or female gender. Such conditions are more common than is generally perceived, affecting up to 2 per cent of the population (Preves 2003).

The core of the Church's teaching on sexuality and on the roles that are appropriate for the different sexes is grounded in, if not based upon, an acceptance of the statement in Genesis 1.27: 'So God created humankind in his image, in the image of God he created them; male and female he created them.' The Church's ethical teaching and discipline depends then on the ability to define and recognize two sexes, male and female; to assign appropriate roles to each; and to define their appropriate behaviour. Throughout the current debate over homosexuality this ability is not generally questioned. For example, Peter Akinola, Archbishop of Nigeria, has written: 'God created two persons – male and female. Now the world of homosexuals has created a third – a homosexual, neither male nor female or both male and female – a strange, two-in-one human' (Akinola 2003).

From a scientific viewpoint, the description of a homosexual as 'a strange, two-in-one human' is highly questionable, yet it is not unfair, by definition, as a description of intersexuals. The existence of intersexuality confounds the tidy categories that some Christian ethicists and church leaders work with and challenges us all to think more deeply about the God-given nature of our sexuality, yet medically a good deal is known about the various conditions that are grouped under the broad heading of intersexuality. In many ways, then, the condition of intersexuality is an interesting one to 'think with' in the context of the contemporary debate about the ethics of homosexuality. In particular, it draws our attention to the complexity and diversity involved in the development of human sexuality. It reminds us that as human beings our identity (especially our sexual identity) is a consequence of our bodily existence, not simply our mental existence; and it also provides a salutary reminder that in the process of ethical discernment, close attention must be paid to the scientific and medical evidence – where it is available. Finally, a consideration of intersexuality draws us into the dilemmas and difficulties that face both doctors and individual patients in handling an individual's sexual identity and choices.

There is a clear need for such a reminder. This can be seen from the recent discussion document from the House of Bishops, *Some Issues in Human Sexuality: A Guide to the Debate* (2003). For astonishingly in over 300 pages the subject was not discussed; by contrast there is a 29-page discussion of transsexualism. Yet transsexualism has an incidence in Western Europe of around 1 in 10,000 males and 1 in 30,000 females, whereas intersexuality affects 1 in 50 individuals. Such an omission speaks powerfully of an agenda dominated by the particular dynamics of an internal church debate rather than one that seeks to speak to the diversity of actual human experience and the challenges that individuals face.

How then is sex determined; how do we become (biologically) male and female? What can go wrong in the unfolding process of sexual development and what can we, or more accurately, members of the medical profession, do to manage those individuals who are neither clearly male nor female?

# How is sex determined?

The determination of the sex of an individual is the result of a complex sequence of events starting at conception. While it would be impossible to describe all of these within the space of a short essay, and indeed parts of this unfolding sequence of events are not fully understood, we can sketch out three broad stages in the process.

## 1 Chromosomal make-up

The most significant factor in an individual's biological identity is their DNA: their genetic inheritance. Found in the nucleus of every cell in the human body, an individual's DNA is unique to them. This extraordinary information-bearing chemical forms itself into discrete units, known as chromosomes, with different species possessing a different number of such chromosomes. Human beings have within each cell 46 such chromosomes, grouped into 23 pairs. Twenty-two of these pairs, known as autosomes, govern the development of general body characteristics; the remaining pair are the sex chromosomes. For a typical female these are two of the same type (XX) but for a typical male they are of different types (one X, one Y). In genetic shorthand these combinations are written as 46XX and 46XY (known as the karyotype).

In reproduction men and women produce gametes, spermatozoa by men and ova by women. These gametes are produced by cells in the testes and ovaries dividing in half by a process known as meiosis, in which one chromosome from each pair goes to each new cell. Such gametes, therefore, will each contain 23 chromosomes: 22 autosomes and 1 sex chromosome. Ova produced by a woman always have an X chromosome and will have the make-up 23X; spermatozoa produced by a man may have an X or a Y and thus have a make-up of 23X or 23Y.

At conception an ovum and a spermatozoan unite to restore the full chromosome complement. It is the chromosome contribution from the male that will decide whether the new cell is male (46XY) or female (46XX). As the newly formed embryo develops in the uterus the presence of a Y chromosome usually assures male development; the presence of two X chromosomes will usually lead to female development.

## 2 Early response to hormonal influence

The gonads, ovaries in the woman and testes in the man, develop from the same region of the embryo. The critical factor in whether ovaries or testes develop from the undifferentiated gonads is the presence of a Y chromosome. When a Y chromosome is present, testes will develop;

when it is absent, ovaries will develop. This is a critical period for sexual development, for early in the intrauterine life of the male embryo a number of hormones (chemical messenger substances that circulate through the body) are produced by the testes. Two of these hormones are particularly important:

- testosterone, which causes the male genitalia to develop;
- Mullerian Inhibiting Factor (MIF), which suppresses the growth of female genitalia.

Without either of these hormones, external female characteristics will develop.

However, the process of masculine development also relies on the ability of the embryonic tissues to respond to testosterone and MIF. This ability to respond is known as end-organ response and, in some cases, the capacity to respond to testicular hormones is absent.

## 3   Later response to the intrauterine environment

To enable the sex hormones produced by the fetus (testosterone and MIF for the male and oestrogen for the female) to have a proper effect it is vital that no other conflicting hormonal or other influence is present. Inappropriate factors present in the intrauterine environment, such as other hormones or chemicals, can lead to atypical development.

These are simply three of the many stages that make up the complete sequence of human sexual development, but they should be sufficient to enable us to understand how some of the principal intersexual states can occur.

# Examples of atypical development

Abnormal developments can occur at any of these three stages, producing some of the many variants of atypical development.

## 1   Chromosomal make-up

Occasionally, due to abnormal development of the gamete or to abnormal fusion of the gametes, a fetus may be conceived with an abnormal set of chromosomes. In most cases this makes viable development of the fetus impossible, but there are a handful of exceptions. Perhaps the most commonly known such condition is the person with Down's syndrome, who possesses three copies of chromosome 21 (trisomy). Other exceptions relate to abnormalities of the sex chromosomes: one chromosome may be missing (45X0) leading to Turner syndrome (the combination 45Y0 is never found and is probably lethal, causing death at an early stage of development). Three sex chromosomes may be present: 47XXX, known as super-female; 47XYY, known as super-male; or 47XXY, which is known as Klinefelter's syndrome.

Typical males have one X and one Y chromosome; typical females have two Xs. As the name suggests there is little ambiguity about the biological sex of 'super-males' and 'super-females' and indeed their genetic condition may go undetected. However, this is clearly not the case with Klinefelter's syndrome (XXY), for they combine the female make-up (XX) and the male make-up (XY). Indeed they would seem to fit Akinola's description of being 'both male and female' exactly.

The incidence of Klinefelter's syndrome is about 1 in 800 of apparent male births. Typically these children develop as males although they have poor muscle development and are less boisterous and more sensitive than their normal brothers. Penis size may be reduced. After puberty the testes atrophy with failure to produce spermatozoa; there is also a reduction in libido and sexual activity. Significant gynaecomastia (breast enlargement) is common.

True hermaphrodites, that is, individuals who develop both ovarian and testicular tissue, either as separate gonads or with both types of tissue in the same organ, are far less common than people with Klinefelter's, especially in the northern hemisphere. Most of these are apparently normal female karyotype (46XX), although a substantial number have mosaic patterns, that is, their bodies are composed of a mixture with some cells of the body showing one pattern and some another. Such mosaic pictures may be 46XX/46XY, 46XY/47XXY; others are less common. A male karyotype 46XY is also possible, but very rare. Depending on proportions of hormones from each type of tissue, maleness or femaleness will predominate, although in the majority of cases a uterus and vagina will be present.

## 2  Failure of end-organ response

We opened our chapter with an example of end-organ response – the case of Helen suffering from AIS. Such individuals have a male karyotype (46XY) and develop testes. These testes produce testosterone and MIF, but the tissues of the body will not respond to testosterone, and so male sexual organs do not develop. However, the response to MIF is normal, and so the development of female sexual organs is suppressed. The result is a person with the outward form of a pre-pubescent girl; but there are no internal female organs and the vagina is short. The testes remain undescended inside the body, in the place where ovaries are usually found.

At the time when puberty might be anticipated there is poor breast development and, as the uterus is absent, menstruation does not occur.

## 3  Late response to inappropriate factors in the intrauterine environment

The classic example of this type of condition is known as adrenogenital syndrome. As well as the hormones adrenalin and cortisol, the adrenal glands also produce testosterone. An inherited defect in the production chain for cortisol in certain female fetuses can lead to excessive amounts of testosterone being produced. If this occurs then at birth the child will have a masculine appearance with ambiguous or male-looking genitalia. Soon after birth some of these children develop life-threatening crises due to salt loss and urgent medical intervention may be required. Even in later life the genital organs remain somewhat masculine in appearance, with an enlarged clitoris and fusion of the outer part of the vagina, which can make sexual intercourse impossible.

## Management of intersexual conditions

The management options for the four examples cited above are broadly as follows:

### Klinefelter's syndrome

Because of the presence of male genitalia at birth these children are usually brought up as males. As already described, they are less aggressively masculine than most boys of their age. Libido is low, and those who do marry women find they are infertile. Osteoporosis (reduction in bone density predisposing to fracture) may occur and breast enlargement (gynecomastia) is common.

There are three management options. The first is to enhance masculinity with drugs such as androgens and Viagra. Surgery may be possible to enhance the size of the penis. Bilateral mastectomy will remove unwanted breast tissue. Except for some cases involving mosaicism the infertility is untreatable.

The second option is to allow the person to change to a female gender. The penis can be removed or reduced in size and the testes removed. An artificial vagina may be created. Facial hair is scanty but can be removed by electrolysis. Oestrogens can be given to enhance breast growth and produce general feminine characteristics.

The third option is simply to do nothing.

## True hermaphrodite

The management of this condition is based on the suitability of the external genital organs for life in a particular gender. Removal of inappropriate gonads, surgical correction and ongoing hormonal support is used in an attempt to steer development into a male or female pattern.

## Androgen Insensitivity Syndrome (AIS)

As explained, these individuals have a male karyotype (46XY) but appear female at birth. At puberty there is poor breast development but menstruation does not occur, and this is usually the reason for seeking medical advice. On examination there will be a short vagina and no uterus. The testes are usually found in the abdomen but sometimes have partially descended.

The management usually entails the removal of the testes (because there is a 5 per cent risk of cancerous change in later life), and oestrogen therapy to promote breast development and other female characteristics.

## Adrenogenital syndrome

Adrenogenital syndrome in the newborn can be a life-threatening condition and requires urgent treatment within days of birth. Cortisone is given to suppress adrenal activity. The child may go through a series of surgical procedures to reduce clitoral size and reconstruct typical female genitalia.

In rehearsing the basic management options available to the surgeon or physician in their treatment of those with such conditions, we are of course only relating part of the story. For such individuals the decision to become 'more' like one gender than the other or indeed, in the face of what can be realized surgically, to remain in a more ambiguous gender, is one of huge psychological consequence. It has lifetime repercussions for a person's sense of identity and autonomy and their ability to relate to others. Such decision-making is routinely fraught and does not bring the sort of easy resolution that some Christian commentators seem to believe possible. As mentioned above, *Some Issues in Human Sexuality* does not touch on the issue of intersexuality, let alone the management options. It does however briefly mention true hermaphroditism. Yet here the discussion is short, merely endorsing the breezy assertion made by an earlier rather superficial treatment of the issue, namely that: 'Hermaphroditism is generally treated in early childhood by surgery and hormone therapy whereby the patient is assigned an unambiguous phenotype of either male or female.' As if this were all that needed to be said. That is far from being the case.

# Problems for theological reflection

Many intersexuals have undergone significant genital surgery; have impaired sexual function; are infertile; and in some sense 'could have been/could have decided to be' the other sex. The current scientific and medical knowledge about intersexuality and the experience of intersexuals themselves therefore raises a whole host of questions about the relationship between sexuality and personal identity. Questions which, while pressing and practical for the individual in question, have profound theological and ethical implications. In what follows I have pursued four such questions:

- Can the rigid division of humanity into male and female still be upheld?
- If the Church is to make certain roles gender dependent, and declare that those who cross these barriers commit sin, how are these genders to be determined?
- If a person has an ambiguous gender should that person be permitted to choose what gender to adopt, or to remain ambiguous?
- Do these factors have any relevance to the debate over same-sex relationships?

The most fundamental of these questions is whether a rigid division of humanity into male and female, which seems to underpin much ethical discussion, can still be upheld. Perhaps because the issue of intersexuality has not been properly addressed within recent ethical discussions about sexuality, the fundamental character of this question has often been persistently avoided.

## Created male or female?

The Christian understanding of sex rests uncompromisingly on Genesis 1.27: 'So God created humankind in his image, in the image of God he created them; male and female he created them.' But, inevitably, the theological and ethical implications of this foundational statement have been worked out in the light of contemporary cultural knowledge and scientific understanding of maleness and femaleness. Thus, for example, throughout much of the Christian era, this text from Genesis was supplemented by Aristotle's understanding which, in effect, conceived of females as 'deficient' or 'lesser' males.

Much of the current debate about gender and sexuality assumes that there is an absolute or rigid division of the human race into two sexes. So for example in its discussion of transsexualism, the authors of *Some Issues in Human Sexuality*, state:

> Furthermore, as the creation narratives in Genesis I and 2 make clear, the basic form in which human beings are created by God to relate to him in this way is as male or female . . . This means that, from the Christian perspective, it is impossible to conceive of a person as a kind of abstract soul . . . To be a human person is to exist bodily as either male or female and to relate to God and other people as such.
>
> (House of Bishops Group 2003, 7.4.5, p. 244)

One can heartily agree that human persons are bodies and not abstract souls, but on purely scientific grounds it is simply impossible to adhere to an absolute or rigid division of the human race into male and female. Such a division is of course broadly useful, and probably around 98 per cent of the population can be categorized in this way (Preves 2003). However, the remaining 2 per cent do not fit neatly into either category; if a rigid division is to be maintained these people will have to be arbitrarily allocated a gender and instructed to act in a role for which they are not fully suited and in which they may not feel comfortable. Furthermore, at least if taken at face value, this rigid division implies that intersexual persons cannot have a proper relationship with God or other people, as they cannot properly exist bodily as male or female.

While the management of intersexuality is evolving, scientific knowledge concerning many of the basic conditions (e.g. Klinefelter's syndrome) has been available for several decades. Yet the Church's public thinking about sexuality could be perceived to permanently exclude the 2 per cent of the population who do not easily fit the simple and rigid categories available. The case of intersexuality reveals challenges for both the Church's ethical thinking and its pastoral theology. The Church should of course treat scientific progress with caution and not rely on lines of approach which may later be refuted. Nevertheless, the Church's response to the discoveries of Copernicus and Galileo is not one that should be repeated.

## Determining gender

Whether one is male or female is of course of particular significance to the Church in its approach to marriage, and for some within the Christian community, ordination to the offices of priest and bishop. But, if the Church is to make certain roles gender dependent, and declares that those who cross these barriers commit sin, how are these genders to be determined?

Medically, the sex of an individual is usually decided by a birth attendant (doctor, midwife, friend or relative) within seconds of delivery.

Two categories are permitted (male and female) and the initial verdict is rarely challenged. In cases of ambiguity, or where problems arise soon after birth, the initial diagnosis may be altered. The second point at which this diagnosis is likely to be challenged is at puberty, following investigations into the failure to menstruate and infertility.

However, the legal definition of sex depends on chromosomal analysis; and this is the definition used in competitive sport where possession of a Y chromosome prevents individuals from competing as women. This definition is also used in marriage disputes, mostly commonly in the United States of America where various States have passed 'Defence of Marriage' Acts.

The injustice to intersexual people caused by this type of ruling is obvious. A person with AIS, who has the outward appearance of a woman and has been brought up in and accepted a female role, could be denied marriage to a man because her karyotype is uniformly 46XY. The same would apply to a true hermaphrodite with 46XX/46XY mosaicism but brought up as a woman. Moreover, it could be argued with equal validity that the possession of two X chromosomes allows the diagnosis of female to be made. In that case those with Klinefelter's syndrome (47XXY) could be classed as both males (XY) and females (XX), and could be allowed to be married to a man or to a woman.

In the USA cases have occurred where a surviving spouse's rights over their partner's estate have been denied because of the results of chromosome analysis. The other side of the coin was revealed in Texas, a State that recognizes only heterosexual unions, where a lesbian couple were able to marry because one was a male-to-female transsexual and hence had a 46XY karyotype. This would also be allowable if one of the parties had AIS.

Similar problems with curious and arbitrary rulings arise over the question of ordination. If, as some argue, it is impossible for a woman to be ordained priest or bishop and validly act as eucharistic president, we are entitled to ask what part of being a woman renders ordination invalid. Is it the chromosomal make-up? In that case those with 46XY but AIS, which has left them with a typical female form, could be ordained. Problems will arise over Klinefelter's (47XXY) and hermaphrodites with male appearance but female (46XX) or mosaic (46XX/46XY) karyotype. There will always be a problem over mosaicism – what percentage of cells must be 46XY rather than 46XX to justify the assignment of male status?

It could, of course, be argued that such cases are the 'exceptions that prove the rule'. Conversely, it could equally be argued that such cases are illustrative and reveal something lacking in our understanding of sex that draws us towards making clearer distinctions than reality permits.

# Choice in the face of ambiguity

If a person has an ambiguous gender should that person be permitted to choose what gender to adopt, or to remain ambiguous?

In the past those found to be hermaphrodite were allowed some degree of choice in the determination of their sex. Thus, in the twelfth century Peter the Chanter wrote:

> The church allows a hermaphrodite, that is, someone with the organs of both sexes, capable of either active or passive functions – to use the organ by which s/he is most aroused or the one to which s/he is most susceptible. If s/he is more active, s/he may wed as a man, but if s/he is more passive s/he may marry as a woman. If however s/he should fail with one organ, the use of the other can never be permitted, but s/he must be perpetually celibate to avoid any similarity to the role inversion of sodomy, which is detested by God.  (quoted in Preves 2003, p. 36)

The medieval Church had a more open view of sexual differences, recognizing more easily than we today that an absolute divide between male and female is not possible. Sadly, some of this tolerance was lost in the modern period when sexuality became a medical matter and surgical 'corrections' became available.

There can be three reasons to treat intersexuality medically or surgically. The first is that the condition is immediately life-threatening. The best example of this is congenital adrenogenital syndrome at birth. Failure to treat with cortisone can lead to death within weeks. The correctness of such decisions is obvious. The second reason is that the condition is life-threatening in the long term. This is usually because anomalous gonads have a higher risk than normal gonads of developing cancerous change. Careful assessment of the degree and timing of this risk is important; for example, if there is a 5 per cent risk of cancerous change in a gonad in middle age there may be no need to undertake surgical removal in childhood before an individual can make a personal decision. Third, there may be cosmetic surgery and/or medical treatment to bring the appearance closer to a male or female stereotype. Such procedures are often performed in two or more stages throughout childhood. This is done at the behest of the parents or accepted by them after medical advice; again the individual is not usually given a personal choice.

However, many intersex people are unhappy with the way that decisions were made for them in early life and at being thrust into a gender role in which they do not feel comfortable. Furthermore, such an approach has often been accompanied by a lack of information or even misinformation about the nature of their condition. A recent study (Preves 2003), which interviewed 37 intersexual adults, found that those who underwent medical sex assignment in their childhood (that is, without their consent) experienced consistently negative and confusing messages about their identities. In particular three themes were commonly reported:

- these people knew that they were objects of medical interest and treatment;
- they knew that they were not to be told what was wrong with them, or why they were receiving medical treatment;
- they were to accept that such procedures were in their best interests and should remain uncontested and undisclosed.

All members of this group spoke frequently of wanting autonomy over their bodies. Feelings of shame were common and most intense in those who had had recurring medical examinations or treatments to impose conformity on ambiguous sexual anatomy. Relating to other inter-sexuals with whom they could discuss these problems led to feelings of relief, acceptance and pride about this difference in their identities. The majority (84 per cent) were sexually active. Of these, half (46 per cent) engaged in sexual activity with partners living in the same gender role, that is, had relationships that would be classed as homosexual on the basis of outward appearance and the gender role that had already been allocated (Preves 2003).

If sex is God-given these individuals ought then to have the right to remain sexually ambiguous, and neither Church nor society should force them into a particular role. To do so is to define intersexuality as an illness rather than a variation and to maintain that, to be healthy, an individual must conform in every way to typical male or female gender, that is, chromosomally, anatomically, physiologically, psychologically and in behaviour.

## The gay debate

As yet no underlying medical explanation has been found for homo-sexual orientation in genetically and phenotypically normal males and females. Research results that are at present inconclusive include:

- *Twin and adoption studies.* Monozygotic twins (those developing from a single fertilized ovum) are more likely to have identical sexual orientation than are dizygotic twins (those developing from two separate ova).
- *Chromosome studies.* Some studies suggest that a predisposition to male homosexuality may be linked to a gene located on part of the X chromosome (Xq28).

- *Prenatal hormonal exposure*. Homosexuality has been linked with male hormone exposure in female fetuses, and in excessive female hormone exposure in male fetuses.
- *Neuroanatomical differences*. It has been claimed there are anatomical differences in two separate parts of the brain (the hypothalamus and the suprachiasmatic nucleus) in homosexual and in heterosexual men, the findings in male homosexuals being closer to the female pattern.

It must be stressed that none of the studies described above are conclusive, and all are contested. Nevertheless most authorities are confident that a medical explanation for same-sex attraction will eventually be found.

However, the matters brought up by our exploration of intersexuality do have some broader application to the debate on homosexuality. The existence of intersexual states means that we cannot with integrity accept the division of the human race into 'pure' lines of male and female, conforming in all ways (chromosomes, anatomy, physiology, hormones, psychology) to one or other pattern. Nature, and by implication God, has provided much more variety than that. There has been a systematic, if well-intentioned, attempt to force intersexual people to conform to this rigid view of humanity. Yet, unsurprisingly, because such intervention has routinely been imposed upon rather chosen by the individuals concerned, there has been a high failure rate and it has been experienced as uniformly traumatic. As we have seen, it can also become ridiculous, as when chromosome analysis becomes the basis of marriage law.

Intersexuality has not been properly addressed within recent ethical discussions about sexuality. One consequence of this omission has been that the rigid and polarized view that humans are clearly and discretely either male or female has gone unchallenged. The case of the intersexual draws us back to the underlying and central importance of the person, made in the image of God. Yet if we were to accept that intersexual people have the right to choose an adopted gender, or to remain sexually ambiguous, and furthermore are free to choose the sexual orientation in which they feel most comfortable and fulfilled and in which they have the most to give, can homosexual people be denied the same rights? Of course, such a denial might need to be reviewed in the future if and when medical science has revealed the causes of homosexual orientation. But even if no cause for homosexual orientation were found, are we to accept freedom of choice for one group but not for another when the difference between them may be as little as a minor degree of chromosome mosaicism?

Alternatively, we could accept that sexual anatomy, physiology, psychology and orientation is a wide and varied field, with clustering of the majority around the two points of conventional male and female but by no means confined to these. In Genesis 2.18 it is recorded that God said, 'It is not good that the man shall be alone; I will make him a helper as his partner.' God then offered the man every animal and bird as a helper to be his partner, and the man rejected them. God then offered him the woman, whom he had made by division of the man, and the man accepted her. That choice was Adam's, not God's – human, not divine; should it not remain so?

# References

Akinola, P., 'Why I object to homosexuality', *Church Times*, 4 July 2003.

House of Bishops Group, *Some Issues in Human Sexuality: A Guide to the Debate*, Church House Publishing, London, 2003.

Preves, S. E. *Intersex and Identity: The Contained Self*, Rutgers University Press, New Brunswick, 2003.

# 9

# Psychology and orientation:
# being human within culture and history

ARNOLD BROWNE

Because it is unlikely that consensus will emerge quickly, the question of the limits of diversity is central to the Anglican debate about sexuality. How far is it acceptable for those with different views to remain in communion with one another? Accordingly, the Lambeth Commission on Communion was set up to consider ways in which understanding could be enhanced while serious differences of opinion threatened the life of the worldwide Anglican Church. In its Windsor Report (2004), the Commission notes the importance of 'distinguishing acceptable and unacceptable forms of diversity' (paragraph 71) and offers what it suggests are obvious examples of the latter:

> It has never been enough to say that we must celebrate or at least respect 'difference' without further ado. Not all 'differences' can be tolerated. (We know this well enough in the cases of, say, racism or child abuse; we would not say, 'some of us are racists, some of us are not, so let's celebrate our diversity'.) This question is frequently begged in current discussions. (paragraph 89)

However, it is worth asking just what it is we know 'well enough' when we consider the chosen examples of 'racism or child abuse'. Psychology, which seeks to understand why people do the things they do, can help us here. Particularly so when we recognize 'the importance of the cross-cultural approach to psychology' and that 'psychologists are now moving on to the task of understanding the reasons behind the similarities and differences we observe in different cultures' (Eysenck 2004, p. ix).

## 'The cases of, say, racism or child abuse'

In 1772 Thomas Thompson, chaplain of Cape Coast Castle, the shore headquarters in Africa (in present-day Ghana) of the British involvement in the slave trade, published his *The African trade for negro slaves shown to be consistent with the principles of humanity and with the laws of revealed religion*. Thompson had no difficulty in demonstrating that slavery was consistent with the Bible, and he described unchristian Africans as 'of as dark a mind as complexion'. Twenty years later, the Archbishop of Canterbury himself, John Moore, came out in support of the continuation of the slave trade as a legitimate occupation for a Christian.

On 28 April 1885 another Archbishop of Canterbury, Edward White Benson, spoke in the House of Lords on the Criminal Law Amendment Bill. He advocated the raising of the age of consent for girls from 13 to 16: 'Was the law, then, to allow a child under that age, who was not held responsible in other areas of daily life, to be responsible for handing herself over for self-ruin?' However, Benson was content that girls under 16, although 'the earliest age at which the law recognized the right of girls to exercise independent responsibility', should nevertheless be allowed to be married: 'because in the case of marriage there was the consent of the parents, who handed over their child to the care of a man who undertook to maintain and protect her'. Benson thus supported the arranged marriage of girls acknowledged to be too young to make their own decisions. Most of us would now be uneasy with this as an unacceptable subordination of women, but many of us might further feel that parents who 'handed over their child to the care of a man' were abusing her.

Benson was a former headmaster and his son recorded that all his old pupils 'agree in thinking that he believed in and used physical punishment far more than was necessary' (Benson 1923, p. 52). Benson's savage flogging of boys was indeed something he believed in, and it has clear scriptural support: 'Those who spare the rod hate their children' (Proverbs 13.24). However, many of us now would think it a form of child abuse.

It may be that we now know 'well enough' that racism and child abuse are not to be tolerated. However, we must also be careful to acknowledge not only that Christians have held very different views about appropriate relationships between races and about proper treatment of children but also that beliefs and practices which we would regard as racist and abusive have been justified by an appeal to the Bible. This awareness can help us to appreciate the importance of the insights of Richard Hooker, the great sixteenth-century Anglican theologian. He argued that it was not self-evident from scripture but 'must be by reason founde out' which of the examples and precedents in scripture are always to be followed, and which 'the Church hath power to alter' when 'it manifestly appears to her that change of times have clearly taken away the very reasons of God's first institution' (*Laws* III.ix.1; VII.v.8). In our Christian understanding of what it means to be human we must accept the challenge of relating the real insights that we gain from cultural, historical and scientific study to our responsible reading of scripture.

There is a tendency to polarization and to simplification in the current debate. However, the evidence will not allow us to say, for example, that Christianity has always taken a positive view of racial equality and of children's rights on the one hand but a negative view of homosexuality on the other. In fact, Christian understanding of what it means to be human has connected ideas of race and status with conceptions of gender and sexuality in ways which suggest that what we now claim to know 'well enough' may yet yield to a new consensus.

## Race and sexuality

Writing not long before the birth of Jesus, the Roman historian Sallust lamented Rome's decline into a state of moral depravity. He and his fellow Romans laid the blame for this deterioration on an exposure to the ways of the Greeks, and saw this in terms of a perversion of natural desires. For Sallust there was an obvious connection between beginning 'to admire statues, pictures, and sculptured vases' and finding that men were being penetrated by other men, that 'men endured things done to women' (*Conspiracy of Catiline* 11–13). Modern historians are not all in agreement with Cato and Sallust that homosexual intercourse became a Roman practice only after the upper classes became Hellenized, but the connection that they make between what they regard as an alien race and what they consider perverted sexuality is persistent in human culture and history.

Similarly, the prohibition in Leviticus 18.22, 'You shall not lie with a male as with a woman' (see Leviticus 20.13), is part of a Holiness Code (Leviticus 17—26) that distinguishes the practices of the people of Israel from the customs of other races: 'You shall not do as they do in the land of Egypt, where you lived, and you shall not do as they do in the land of Canaan, to which I am bringing you' (Leviticus 18.3). In Judaism of the Roman period, homoeroticism therefore became associated with non-Jewish activities. This is reflected in Paul's association of idolatry with both male and female homoeroticism in Romans 1.18–32 and is evident, for example, in the rabbinic commentary on Leviticus. Here too the prohibition of homosexual practice is extended to females as well as males on the grounds that this also is an alien practice of Canaanites and Egyptians: 'And what did they do? A man married a man and a woman a woman' (*Sifra Leviticus* 18.3). Just as the Romans represented male and female (see, for example, Ovid *Heroides* 15; *Tristia* 2.365) homoeroticism as a Greek phenomenon, foreign to Roman customs, so their Jewish contemporaries represented it as Gentile, foreign to the practices of Israel.

These attitudes are by no means confined to the ancient world. In 1819 the House of Lords decided in favour of two teachers, Miss Woods and Miss Pirie, who had sued for libel because they had been accused of homoeroticism. In their favour was the fact that one of their accusers, a Miss Cumming, was coloured and from India. It was thought by some of their Lordships that while such perverted sexuality might exist in India, it was inconceivable that a British woman could be capable of such an act. Before we distance ourselves as free from such outdated prejudices, we should consider our response to not dissimilar views being expressed today. There are voices to be heard which suggest that homosexuality is a western phenomenon alien to the Islamic world. Equally it is sometimes said that homoeroticism is un-African, which is why Anglican Christians on that continent cannot be expected to share the accepting attitudes of some of their brothers and sisters in North America and Europe. However, the evidence suggests that these claims are no better grounded than those of Cato and Sallust who represented homosexuality as quite un-Roman but thoroughly Greek. Indeed, recent reports to Mariam Omar of the BBC's Swahili Service from prisons in Kenya and Zanzibar suggest that male rape is routinely used for subjugation, punishment and torture, precisely because of a macho culture in which homosexuality is never discussed, and the victims of male rape see themselves as having been shamed by being treated as women.

This interweaving of attitudes to sexuality and to race suggests that it is culturally and historically inappropriate to argue that while we may now be confused about the former we have always been clear about the latter. It is worth reminding ourselves that connections between racial and sexual purity are made in the scriptures themselves, most strikingly in the account in Numbers 25 of the slaughter of Zimri and Cosbi, an Israelite man and the Midianite woman he brought 'into his family' (25.6). Phinehas the priest slaughters the couple, piercing with one stroke of his spear the two of them together, seemingly in the act of sexual intercourse. This act stops a plague, which the chapter associates with sexual relations with foreign women who invite sacrifices to their gods, and so Phinehas is commended, 'because he was zealous for his God, and made atonement for the Israelites' (25.13). This zeal of Phinehas was used as a significant example by many Jews in the time of Jesus and was associated with Jewish nationalism (see especially 1 Maccabees 1.23–26; Sirach 45.23–25). Writing in the first century AD the Jewish historian Josephus, who retells at length the incident recorded in Numbers 25 (*Antiquities* 4.131–55), is typical of most of his contemporaries in emphasizing the passages in the scriptures (see also Exodus 34.15–16) that forbid racially mixed marriages. In line with Genesis 34.14, which makes clear that Jacob's daughter Dinah could not be married to a man with a foreskin, Josephus says explicitly that circumcision was instituted so that Abraham's descendants should be 'unmixed with others' (*Antiquities* 1.192). Earlier in the same century Philo had described circumcision as a means of ensuring 'that no foreign seed should be sown' (*Question on Genesis* 3.61). This social function of circumcision makes all the more striking not only Paul's insistence that the true descendants of Abraham can be either circumcised or uncircumcised (Romans 4.9–12) but also his acceptance of marriages between believers and unbelievers (1 Corinthians 7.12–16).

Although the New Testament does not maintain any connection between racial and sexual purity, it has persisted in Christian societies. South Africa in the period of Apartheid is an obvious example, with the Immorality Act and the Prohibition of Mixed Marriage Act, repealed in 1985. But there are other examples. In nineteenth-century England 'Prince' Peter Lobengula, supposedly the son of the king of the Matabele tribe and the centre of attention in the 'Savage South Africa' tour of 1899, became engaged to a white woman, Kitty Jewel. The moral outrage in the press was such that, sad to record, they had to be married not in church but in a civil ceremony. Following the American Civil War and the emancipation of the slaves there was such an obsession with 'miscegenation' that forty US States prohibited interracial marriages (defined, for example, in South Carolina as the marriage of a white person with any 'person who shall have one eighth or more of Negro blood'). Interracial marriage was criminalized in some States until as recently as the 1960s.

Far from knowing well enough that racism is a difference that can never be tolerated, the Christian Church has been caught up into the connections between attitudes to race and to sexuality, which have been so persistent in human culture and history. If we allow ourselves to recognize this, then we must be very alert to the possibility that some attitudes to homosexuality being expressed by contemporary Christians are tinged with racism, and be very careful not to collude with them.

## Gender and sexuality

It is sometimes argued that our concept of sexual orientation was unknown in the pre-modern period. However, the evidence suggests instead that in the ancient world people were already categorized by their lifelong sexual preferences. The male citizen was expected to be active rather than passive in intercourse, and the free men of Athens saw it as perfectly normal to have not only penetrative intercourse with their wives but also non-penetrative intercrural (between the thighs) intercourse with free boys (see Aeschines, *Against Timarchus* 135; Plato, *Charmides* 155d–e). However, even in erotic painting there is no suggestion that the boys themselves, future citizens of Athens, experienced any sexual desire or satisfaction in these encounters. Sex between men of a similar age was not seen to be an acceptable aspect of male sexuality, and indeed the most despised of men was the *kinaidos*, an effeminate adult male who allowed his body to be penetrated for pleasure by another man (see Aristophanes, *Women at the Thesmophoria* 574–654; Plato, *Gorgias* 494a–495a). The *kinaidos* was seen to transgress the accepted gender distinctions because he was not the penetrator but the penetrated. A treatise wrongly attributed to Aristotle explains the supposed effeminacy of the *kinaidos* in terms of his being as sexually insatiable as a woman, because he is unable to experience a manly erection and the release of ejaculation (*Problemata* 4.26.29–30). This passage associates what it sees as a contradiction of masculinity with inappropriate sexual experience, suggesting that the *kinaidos*' desire to be penetrated could be a consequence of repeated penetration at the time of adolescent 'ripeness'. Similarly, Aristotle himself argues that a disposition to sexual passivity could be created through habituation, 'as in the case of those violated in youth' (*Nichomachean Ethics* 1148b.27–29).

In the Roman world too people could be categorized by their sexual preferences. Again a male citizen was categorized by his taking the active part whatever the gender of the passive partner: 'When your groin bulges, if a servant-girl or an estate-born boy is handy, whom you can jump on right away, would you prefer being ruptured by the swelling? Not me, I want my sex ready and accessible' (Horace, *Satires* 1.2.114–19). Again too there were those who were seen to have a life-long propensity to deviate from what were seen as the natural patterns of active male and passive female sexuality. For example, in the second century AD Soranos of Ephesos discusses what he sees as the mental disease of soft or passive men (*On Chronic Diseases* 4.9). He considers passive males in anal intercourse to be unnatural (*non . . . ex natura*) while presuming their penetrating partners to be healthy (*On Acute Diseases* 3.18; SS180f). For Soranos, what he sees as male effeminacy results from allowing lust free reign. He compares these diseased passive men with *tribades*, women who take the active part in same-sex relationships. And just as the active partners in male–male relationships are considered to be healthy, so too the passive partners in female–female relationships are not seen to be diseased (*On Chronic Diseases* 4.9; S132). It is only the active women who are seen to be unnatural. Seneca the Younger describes those who 'even rival men in their lusts although born to be passive'. These women 'having devised so deviant a type of shamelessness, enter men' (*Epistulae Morales* 95.20).

Modern psychology emphasizes the importance of distinguishing between sexual orientation and sexual behaviour. It is often argued that until the nineteenth century sexuality was discussed only in terms of sexual acts, and that there were no systems of classification according to different sexual desires. However, although they did not think of sexual orientation as degrees of sexual attraction to men or women, it is clear that in ancient Rome, as in ancient Greece, there was much categorizing of human sexuality according to the complexities of different desires. This becomes particularly clear from astrological texts. In the second century AD Ptolemy categorized the Moon and Venus as feminine, as more moist, and the Sun, Saturn, Jupiter and Mars as masculine, being more dry. People, like planets, have an assigned gender, but both are potentially volatile. Planetary positions at the time of birth can therefore cause sexual behaviour appropriate to the opposite sex (*Tetrabiblos* 1.6; SS19–20). Of course for Ptolemy natural (*kata physin*) male behaviour is active and natural female behaviour is passive (1.12; S33). Interestingly, Ptolemy's astrology not only distinguished between active and passive sexualities but also accounted for being attracted to someone in terms of their age, race and social standing. In the fourth century AD Julius Firmicus Maternus' astrological system was sufficiently complex to account not only for homoeroticism, which he considered a reprehensible transgression of gender boundaries, but also for such categories as that of the man who desires to marry a masculine woman and have children from her (*Matheseos libri viii* 3.11.11) or of the Virago, who could be married and have relationships with men as well as women (3.5.23).

That the term 'homosexual' was coined in 1869 is indicative of the development in the nineteenth century of the concept of two different sexual orientations, conceived in terms of attraction to someone of the same or of the opposite sex. If in the twenty-first century we are recognizing that the spectrum of desires may be more complex, then we have been preceded by the ancient Greeks and Romans. We may also be following them in acknowledging that there are many interacting factors, biological and psychological, hereditary and experiential, determining what we now call 'orientation'. Of course our emphases are different from theirs. Many of us would not see the categories of active and passive to be fundamental, and we might be uneasy about their linking the former to men and the latter to women. Not many of us would be followers of ancient astrology, and our understanding of biology does not distinguish between moist and insatiable women and dry and satisfied men.

The biblical writers, like the ancient Greeks and Romans, also held that appropriate sexual behaviour should conform to an understanding of the role of men as naturally active and of women as naturally passive (see especially the discussion of Leviticus 18.22; 20.13, and Romans 1.18–32 in Chapters 2 and 3 above). Despite the differences that we have seen between ancient and modern explanations of orientation, this connection between approved sexual behaviour and accepted gender roles shows considerable powers of persistence. Freud himself argued that 'a great part of the male inverted [homosexuals] have retained the psychic character of virility, that proportionately they show but little of the secondary character of the other sex, and that they really look for real feminine psychic features in their sexual object' (Freud 1930, p. 8). But from the 1930s, as psychoanalysis moved to the political Right on most issues, homosexuality came to be seen more simplistically in terms of the pathological failure of normal gender development. This is the view made common by the popularizing of psychoanalysis since the 1960s. Female homosexuality is seen to be a stage in growing up through which some women do not develop, and male homosexuals are characterized by their failure to possess proper masculine authority and strength. In this psychoanalytic account of male homosexual intercourse, other men's penises become symbols of this desired male authority and strength. 'And as they're *not* the thing they symbolise, the person is never satisfied, never has enough, often goes from one partner to another' (Skynner and Cleese 1983, p. 257). It is doubtful that these theories are any more scientific than those of the ancient astrologers, and indeed they come very close to ancient Greek ideas about the effeminate and insatiable *kinaidos*.

In 1974 the American Psychological Society voted no longer to classify homosexuality as a mental disorder involving sexual deviation. Since then psychologists have widened their approach to the origins of sexual orientation to consider the involvement of genetic factors. To date, the balance of evidence suggests that 'sexual orientation may be only modestly influenced by heredity' (Eysenck 2004, p. 88). We are then moving away from the assumption that, since 'opposites attract', homosexuals must be abnormally masculine women and effeminate men. However, the connection between approved sexual behaviour and accepted gender roles can still be traced in some contemporary accounts of homosexuality as a denial of the fundamental experience of 'otherness', which is said to be integral to heterosexual relationships. Of course, debate about the differences between men and women, and the extent to which they are 'essential' or 'constructed', is lively and ongoing. The result of much psychological research seems to be that 'Where differences appear, they are small compared to variation within either sex, and very small compared to differences in the social positioning of men and women' (Connell 2005, p. 47). In any event, it is certainly worth considering whether it is only gender differences that can enable one person to recognize the 'otherness' of their partner's humanity. While it is right to encourage caring and respectful relationships rather than narcissistic and selfish ones, it is not evident either that heterosexual relationships always guarantee respect for the other as equally a person of infinite value in the sight of God or that homosexual relationships inevitably deny this proper sense of 'otherness'.

It is sometimes said that support for faithful homosexual relationships, such as in the recent recognition of civil partnerships, is inevitably undermining of marriage. On the face of it this is a surprising argument, since the social importance of a commitment to one another and a capacity to trust one another are equally recognized both in civil partnerships and in marriage. It seems likely that the real concern of this argument is with the 'undermining' of a view of marriage that emphasizes the difference between the partners in terms of a patriarchal understanding of approved and historical gender roles. It is worth reminding ourselves that the accepted and traditional view of male authority and activity in marriage meant that in the United Kingdom it was only in 1991 that marital rape was recognized as a crime. Before then it was a legal and social impossibility for a man to be guilty of raping or sexually assaulting his wife. This traditional subordination of one partner to the other in marriage is not characteristic of homosexual relationships, where commentators notice more reciprocity, for example in equality of age, education and income. There is then some force to the argument that 'Homosexual masculinity is a contradiction for a gender order structured as modern Western systems are' (Connell 2005, p. 162). This becomes even more clear when we recognize that Freud was right in seeing gay men as no more effeminate than straight men, despite the persistent stereotypes, and when we allow that, given their increasingly observable friendly relationships with women, we can no longer argue that male homosexual development is grounded in an antipathy to the opposite sex. Indeed, the gay community's visibility may partly explain why there are now many heterosexual couples who, because they see their own relationships as reciprocal, do not wish to commit themselves to what they understand to be the patriarchal institution of marriage, but who would gladly commit themselves to one another for life in a civil partnership were that possibility open to them.

The New Testament has some radical things to say about gender, most obviously in Paul's striking statement that 'there is no longer male and female; for all of you are one in Christ Jesus' (Galatians 3.28). In his reading of Adam's fall, Paul sees homosexual acts in terms of the reversal of 'natural' gender roles (Romans 1.26–27). But in his instructions to married couples who are part of God's new creation in Christ he moves forward from the world of male activity and female passivity: 'for the wife does not have authority over her own body, but the husband does; likewise the husband does not have authority over his own body, but the wife does' (1 Corinthians 7.4).

It is important that we recognize the complex connections between our conceptions of gender and our attitudes to sexuality. It could be that it is the failure to support a faithful and loving homosexual relationship that 'undermines' the equal and mutual relationship of male and female which should characterize Christian marriage.

## Status and sexuality

In pointing out that 'Not all "differences" can be tolerated', the Windsor Report argued that 'We know this well enough in the cases of, say, racism or child abuse'. Until the legalization of male homosexual intercourse in 1967 it could be said that 'we' in the United Kingdom knew 'well enough' that this was a difference that could not be tolerated. We should not forget either that there are Islamic countries where homosexual activity still carries the death penalty or that for over a thousand years, from the sixth century to the nineteenth, Christian societies regularly put homosexuals to death. On 1 February 1816 James Cooper and three of his shipmates from *H.M.S. Africaine* were executed for buggery, and historians have traced the ways in which the increase of prosecutions for sodomy in the period of the Napoleonic wars was linked with fears of heresy, insurrection and rebellion in the wake of the French revolution: 'Extreme hostility to homosexual acts was a relatively recent acquisition for Englishmen in the closing decades of George III's reign' (Burg, 1984, pp. xv–xvi). The explanation seems to be that the sodomite's sexual disorder was seen to represent the social disorder threatened from France. This type of mythology was explicitly used by Heinrich Himmler in a speech made in 1937 outlining his intention to send homosexuals to the death camps: 'I hope finally to have done with persons of this type in the SS, and the increasingly healthy blood which we are cultivating for Germany, will be kept pure'. Here the connection between status and sexuality, conceived in terms of social and sexual dissidence, is most terrifyingly clear.

The world has moved on since then, but it is possible to see how the increasing visibility of the gay community now questions accepted patterns of status, particularly of the power of American and European heterosexual men in the private sphere of their homes and the public sphere of politics, as well as in the economic and military orders by which the world's resources are allocated. These challenges arise 'not necessarily from a partly pacified gay community, but certainly from the situation defined by its presence' (Connell, 2005, p. 220).

Given the clear connections between sexuality and status, it is not surprising that much of the current discussion of the subject is in the language of human rights. In the House of Bishops' discussion document *Some Issues in Human Sexuality* (2003), this way of thinking about sexuality is traced back only as far as 'the Enlightenment discussion about human rights' (5.2.1). However, we should not ignore the antecedents of this secular language in the Judaeo-Christian understanding of human beings as created in the image of God. And Jesus' teaching that 'even the hairs of your head are all counted' (Luke 12.7) is particularly striking in his context within the Roman Empire. Simon Goldhill says of the gladiators in ancient Rome:

> A slave's body had none of the protections of a citizen. A slave, unlike a citizen, had no rights, and could not avoid beatings, brandings, torture and forced sex by his or her own master – and all these were regular features of Roman society in practice. Rape was a punishment for male and female servants, whippings a commonplace. The exposure of the gladiator's flesh and its violent treatment was made possible in Roman eyes because the slave and the criminal were bodies to be used, for punishment, for work – and for entertainment.          (Goldhill 2004, p. 237)

Paul, the Roman citizen, was both conscious of his rights and willing to forgo them in the service of the gospel: 'I have made no use of any of these rights, nor am I writing this so that they may be applied in my case. Indeed, I would rather die than that' (1 Corinthians 9.15). Although a free male, he could describe himself as someone condemned to die in a Roman theatre (1 Corinthians 4.9) and he suffered the 'imprisonments, with countless floggings' (2 Corinthians 11.23) inflicted on the slave.

Recognizing the connections between attitudes to sexuality and status should help us to avoid expressing attitudes that fail to take into account the New Testament's radical questioning of the ideal of the inviolate male citizen with his exclusive rights.

# Conclusion

We have seen some of the ways in which attitudes to sexuality are subtly but persistently interwoven with views of race, gender and status. If we wish unequivocally to proclaim with Paul that 'There there is no longer slave or free, there is no longer Jew or Greek, there is no longer male and female' (Galatians 3.28), then we need to be sensitive to the work of those, including psychologists, who can help us to understand why people behave as they do, in different contexts and periods. It is our Christian responsibility to understand what it means to be human by connecting the insights of scripture and tradition with the realities of our culture and history.

Preaching in Southwark Cathedral on 1 February 2004, Archbishop Desmond Tutu appealed to 'the Jesus I worship' in speaking out passionately against penalization on the grounds of race, gender or sexuality: 'To discriminate against our sisters and brothers who are lesbian or gay on grounds of their sexual orientation for me is as totally unacceptable and unjust as Apartheid ever was.' Realizing that Christians have appealed to scripture to support not only racism but also child abuse, and recognizing for example the radical dissociation of sexuality from race and status which we find in the New Testament, we would do well to heed this prophetic voice.

# References

Benson, A. C., *The Trefoil*, John Murray, London, 1923.

Burg, B. R., *Sodomy and the Pirate Tradition: English Sea Rovers in the Seventeenth-Century Caribbean*, New York University Press, New York, 1984.

Connell, R. W., *Masculinities*, Polity Press, Cambridge, 2nd edn 2005.

Eysenck, M. W., *Psychology: An International Perspective*, Psychology Press, Hove and New York, 2004.

Freud, S., *Three Contributions to the Theory of Sex*, Nervous and Mental Disease Publishing Company, New York and Washington, 4th edn 1930.

Goldhill, S., *Love, Sex and Tragedy: Why Classics Matters*, John Murray, London, 2004.

Hooker, R., *The Folger Library Edition of the Works of Richard Hooker* (7 vols: Gen. Ed. W. Speed Hill), The Belknap Press of Harvard University Press, Cambridge MA, 1977–98.

The Lambeth Commission on Communion, *The Windsor Report 2004*, Anglican Consultative Council, London, 2004.

Skynner, R. and Cleese, J., *Families and How to Survive Them*, Methuen, London, 1983.

# Part 4

# THE WIDER HORIZON

For those who work closely with the interpretation of texts, 'a text without a context becomes a pretext'. Similarly, the ethics of same-sex relationships are all too often discussed without a vision that is attentive to the broader social, political and economic context. This is something we seek to address in this final section. In his chapter, Malcolm Brown argues powerfully that we cannot fully understand the 'gay' debate within the Anglican Communion without an acknowledgement of the workings of the global economy, the doctrine of individual freedom it promotes, and its impact upon self-identity and therefore issues of personal morality. Much of the internal division within the Church ostensibly 'about' same-sex relationships he suggests would be seen more clearly were greater attention to be paid to understanding the tension between social liberalism and economic liberalism, especially within the USA and therefore ECUSA (Episcopal Church in the United States of America).

The prospect of deepening conflict and a lack of co-operation between parts of the Anglican Communion is one that concerns Michael Beasley deeply, for he argues it will have wide-ranging and tragic consequences for HIV/AIDS work in Sub-Saharan Africa. Through the extensive network of congregations and dioceses the Anglican Church is well placed, alongside other churches, to bring practical care and support to societies ravaged by the pandemic. Furthermore, such faith traditions are able to tackle the difficult issue of stigma and promote community life where it is threatened. But the financial and medical support required is jeopardized if church leaders seek to make the 'gay issue' one that divides the Anglican Communion.

Finally, Duncan Dormor develops some of the themes explored by Malcolm Brown in an overview of the ways in which human sexuality has been extensively exploited and integrated into commercial activity, ranging from sex trafficking and sex tourism to the rise of Internet porn-ography and erotic marketing. He highlights the key role of developments central to globalization, like the Internet and large-scale international travel, and argues that western culture itself has become increasingly 'sexualized' with a rapidly growing emphasis on, and legitimation of, recreational sex. This view of sexuality, he argues, is deeply impoverished and inherently demeaning: treating men and women as objects or commodities. It is in light of these developments that Christians should evaluate the counter-cultural request from same-sex couples for the imposition of the discipline and structure traditionally associated with marriage: that of faithfulness, exclusivity and permanence.

# 10

# Sex and the city: economics, morality and counter-cultural living

MALCOLM BROWN

In all the churches' debates about sexuality, we have heard a great deal about living 'counter-culturally' but surprisingly little about the dominant cultural factor of our times, namely, the global market economy, how it influences our perceptions of sexual issues and how we should live in relation to it.

It would be easy to suggest that the poverty and disempowerment experienced by much of the world's population as a result of the current economic system constitutes such a moral outrage that the churches are irresponsible to expend so much energy on questions of sexual behaviour. Indeed, such a case has occasionally been advanced during the current controversies. Let us reject that argument immediately. It is a fallacy to assume that the existence of a great evil renders action to address other questions illegitimate. Moreover, for Christians who believe that spiritual health is at least as significant as physical well-being, a scale of significance which allows global poverty to trump all issues of personal moral conduct is not self-evidently true. Certainly, Christians will want to debate the relative claims of economic injustice versus sexual ethics on their finite time and resources, but that question is not my theme here.

One more caveat before the story really starts. I will point to some apparent connections, and possible correlations, between approaches to economic issues and attitudes to sexuality. It might be assumed that the suggestion of a correlation implies a causal explanation. In other words, I might risk being mistaken for an 'economic determinist' seeking to explain all human behaviour in terms of self-interested responses to economic stimuli. My claims here are more modest. I believe that the churches have been extraordinarily reluctant to examine morality in terms of the demands the economy makes on social relationships and participation. Churches have done much good work on the ethics of (for instance) world trade and debt relief, and have used the Bible very powerfully in doing so. But churches continue to address global ethics and personal morality as if they were rather separate things. I want to begin the process of asking how economic issues might be impinging on the current controversy about sexuality and Christian ethics. There are some interesting connections to be made; but concrete conclusions based on irrefutable evidence must await a bigger research project.

## Economics shaping morality

The churches' tendency to ignore the economic context when addressing personal morality is itself a reflection of the individualistic mindset which the churches often claim to oppose, and of which the market economy is a central icon. It is as if we imagine people struggling with moral dilemmas in a kind of social vacuum, unencumbered by the need to earn a living, provide for families or manage complex compromises. Yet it is clear that economic concerns shape moral reasoning in two main ways. They influence how people weigh their own needs when deciding how to behave, and they shape social assumptions to emphasize some moral virtues over others – even turning old virtues into new vices and vice versa – so that behaviour can be moulded to economic imperatives.

For example, consider attitudes to divorce and remarriage. In a consumer economy, the boundary between aspects of life which are open to personal choice, and those which have hitherto been accepted as 'givens', shifts strongly in the direction of greater choice. The notion that some choices are of a permanent nature, or that a context which ceases to give satisfaction, should be endured rather than swapped for another, becomes strained, naturally influencing views about marriage. The way we talk about one area of our lives spills over into others. Moreover, the last quarter-century has seen an enormous rise in insecurity at work, and reinventing oneself in different employment patterns is encouraged since it is thought to enhance productivity and economic innovation. So small wonder that, after years of marriage, one's partner declares that 'You are not the man/woman I married'. Margaret Thatcher's governments found that economic insecurity created an 'incentive' to work harder but sat awkwardly alongside social conservatism and the celebration of stable families – a combination that David Cameron seems to be rethinking.

One could suggest other examples. The 'morality' of women working outside the home shifted throughout the last century. The declining birth rate between the Wars turned home-making into a moral duty for women. Later, the attractiveness of women workers in certain sectors of the economy (where women with families are seen as less demanding and more compliant than men) has coincided with a degree of moral opprobrium towards women with children who seek welfare benefits rather than working. Nor are the churches immune from the impact of economic change on human priorities. The Sunday Trading legislation has (despite the promise of safeguards) forced many to work on Sundays or face redundancy: Sunday working is one factor cited in surveys of those who have ceased attending churches, or attend less frequently (Richter and Francis 1998).

Making such connections, as I have said, does not mean accepting a dismal economic determinism. But ignoring the influence of people's economic needs, or forgetting the formative power of the economy in shaping social attitudes, risks making facile moral judgements. The economy has always been a significant factor in moulding human behaviour. When Paul preached at Ephesus against images of gods made with human hands (Acts 19.23–41) we can identify with the local silversmiths who saw the threat he posed to their livelihood.

If we accept that economic concerns influence public morality, we should also expect this influence to be covert or not consciously recognized. Part of the genius of capitalism is that it preaches a doctrine of individual freedom while allowing economic freedoms to be exercised only within the narrow parameters that reinforce its own workings. As a simple example, those temples of choice, the supermarkets, offer surprisingly little choice if one turns the question around to ask where, rather than on what, one spends one's money. Shaping moral opinion is a subtle process and, like much in market capitalism, is not controlled from any central point. People are as free to choose their moral stances as to choose their brand of washing powder – but in practice consensuses emerge which place one brand in a commanding position or allow one understanding of morality to become the norm; other choices and other behaviour coming to seem odd, or even deviant. In a consumer economy, the dominant discourses of choice and freedom conceal a considerable degree of conformity and common analysis of where individual interests lie.

Christians are, of course, not immune from wider social pressures but, when we factor in religious belief, things start to get interesting. If there ever was a time when being a good Christian was coterminous with being a good citizen within a Christian State that time has passed. Most Christians now understand their beliefs to be, in some ways, at odds with the prevailing culture around them. The difficulty is that there remains a considerable Christian legacy in the ordering of most western societies, and the interpretation of culture is itself contentious. Virtually all Christians today want to live counter-culturally in some manner. What they cannot agree about is which aspects of contemporary culture are so devilish that they must be opposed.

## Counter-cultural: but which culture?

In practice, there appears to be a real divide between Christians who believe themselves called to witness against contemporary cultural excesses by opposing aspects of sexual diversity and those who attack the perceived injustices of global capitalism. Western Christians rarely seem to combine a strongly anti-gay stance with a critique of the market economy. And this is, at first sight, surprising because there are interesting connections between the social prominence of homosexual lifestyles and the present phase of the consumer market economy.

One persistent economic problem is that, as competition drives down profit margins in key sectors, new sources of profit have to be opened up. Privatization programmes have been driven partly by the desire to realize private profit from areas of life that had once recycled profits (if any) to the State. Profit can also be pursued through what are effectively cartels (e.g. the supermarkets); concentration on sectors where high prices (and hence profit margins) confer status or exclusivity, or targeting social groups where there are reserves of untapped disposable income. This latter stratagem has brought the homosexual community to the attention of business as never before. The 'pink pound' has become an attractive potential market. Homosexuals are less likely than others to have dependent children eating into their disposable incomes. A greater tolerance of homosexual people has enabled them to find ways of expressing themselves materially rather than blending into the background and, as all markets fragment, the gay sector has acquired its own distinctiveness.

Profit has never been especially subservient to morality. Even the most homophobic entrepreneur may hold his nose and target the 'pink pound' if there is serious money to be made there, and the majority of entrepreneurs are probably neutral towards questions of sexuality. Social tolerance in general may have created the initial conditions for a gay market, but it is consumer capitalism which has facilitated the heightened awareness and public prominence of gay and lesbian people today.

## Liberals and conservatives untangled

At this point it is worth exploring the odd usage of the words 'liberal' and 'conservative' in the churches' debate about sexuality. Neither term is often used with much precision, but it does makes some sense to trace the liberal motifs of tolerance and the primacy of conscience among those in the churches who are relaxed about homosexual relationships and to term 'conservative' those who seek to prohibit gay relationships through appeal to sacred texts and long-established traditions. However, when we examine attitudes to the economy, some strange anomalies arise. The market is the quintessentially liberal institution, designed to facilitate the transactions of a society of strangers who share no allegiance to shared texts or traditions. The market is avowedly – almost jubilantly – indifferent to beliefs or morality. Yet scepticism about market institutions, and opposition to market outcomes, is strongest among theological 'liberals' in the West, whereas the theological conservatives, like political conservatives, seem broadly in favour. In general church life, those who are most stridently anti-liberal regarding sexual morality are rarely so vocal about the ethics of market economics, although the market is the ultimate cultural icon of liberal rootlessness and individualism. One might go further and suggest that theological conservatives tend to reflect the agenda of political conservatives who, at least in the last quarter of the twentieth century, combined social conservatism (even authoritarianism) with economic liberalism in an ideologically unresolved mix.

There are real difficulties unravelling the tangled terminology of 'liberal' and 'conservative' – and indeed, 'radical'. But my point is that attitudes to market economics are a touchstone that helps us test the consistency of positions – and which expose the tension in the theological conservatives' claim to be epitomizing counter-cultural discipleship within a liberal society when that society is dominated by a liberal market economy with which they seem strangely at ease.

## American models

The application of economic concepts to analyses of church life becomes even more interesting when we cross the Atlantic. Grace Davie notes how a fundamental market mechanism, Rational Choice Theory, governs the highly competitive religious 'market place' in the United States with various brands of faith offering themselves up to people's consumeristic choices, trading different levels of spiritual 'benefit' for different levels of commitment (Davie 2002). Here, the contradiction of anti-liberal church conservatives gladly embracing the quintessentially liberal institutions of the market economy is even more obvious than in Britain. Some theologians draw this out well. Highly influential on both sides of the Atlantic, and a scourge of 'liberal' theology, the Mennonite-inspired theologian Stanley Hauerwas attacks the implication that to be a good Christian is the same as being a good American. Many of those who fall under his strictures would run a mile from the 'liberal' label yet, in their collusion with culture, that is exactly how he sees them.

Where one speaks from is crucial in any debate. And, considering the disparities of power and ownership within the global economy, certain aspects of the sexuality debate appear in a new light. For example, it has been a real problem to 'liberals' that stridently anti-gay opinions emanate from parts of the African Church as well as from western conservatives. It has been difficult to argue against the former while maintaining the liberal's traditional bias to the poor. True, not all Christians in Africa share the stance of the Archbishop of Nigeria (Desmond Tutu is a good example) and there are many and complex reasons why approaches to theology – and to sexuality – in parts of Africa take the forms they do. But the question of economic perspective is part of the equation to which I shall return.

In the global economy, it is impossible to ignore the sheer concentration of power and influence represented by the United States. The link between American economic might and American culture is crucial. The global economy trades in much more than goods and services – with the flow of capital comes also a flow of culture and ideology. Globalization tends to marginalize local distinctiveness, and it is in the responses of different world cultures to this trend that the moral questions of the day are being worked out.

Writers on the new global politics often reach for historical precedents to illustrate a point. This is risky as history rarely repeats itself so precisely that worthwhile parallels are possible. But the alternative is to treat every political development as if it were a one-off, incapable of being assessed until it has run its course (not an easy moment to discern). The point I want to explore here is how people and societies relate to a potentially overwhelming power on their doorstep. There may be interesting precedents in attitudes to totalitarianism expressed in Britain prior to the Second World War when, of course, the appalling consequences of totalitarianism lay largely in the then-unknown future.

Wherever there is an imbalance of power a question arises about maintaining relationships with the most powerful. In the 1930s George Orwell identified a current of thinking that went beyond the merely expedient. Part of Orwell's case against the appeasement of Hitler (and, later, against Communist fellow-travellers) was the phenomenon of a kind of power-worship, an adulation of the visible exercise of power and a growing doctrine that power equalled moral righteousness. As Orwell knew from his time in the Imperial Police, a people whose economic and cultural autonomy is under threat may respond either by overt resistance, or by embracing the ideology of the oppressor even though it implies a degree of self-denigration.

I say again, the parallels are not precise, but the tendency to embrace all that is American in culture and attitude reflects something more visceral than any realistic assessment of the social questions facing countries such as Britain. Accounts of the Blair government's attitudes to the Bush regime suggest an extraordinary degree of uncritical subservience. American answers to complex social problems are presented as more attractive than European or home-grown ones. Consumer spending, at times, apes American values with (as a simple example) sales of fuel-inefficient 4x4s burgeoning despite their limited appropriateness to UK driving conditions.

My point here is not, of course, that all things American are bad, but that the values and lifestyles of the biggest kid on the block (to use an American idiom!) are often adopted for reasons deeper than genuine applicability to the receiving culture. This is most evident in cases where an indigenous culture is simultaneously nervous about its own identity and desirous of retaining its former influence. The playground metaphor is not inappropriate here. The bullied child is often not so much the loner, happy with their own company, but the timid child who desperately wants to be among the leaders.

## Importing models of church

As Davie has shown, patterns of church life and secularization have taken very different forms in Europe and North America, with most of the worries about church survival falling on the Europeans (Davie 2002). It is hardly surprising that, in church life as in politics, patterns and practices from across the Atlantic are viewed with enthusiasm and even envy from the British perspective.

Although only one factor in Britain's changing ecclesiastical profile, we can certainly map the networking between British church conservatives and their counterparts in the United States. One minor but telling clue, persistent over decades, is the use of the expression 'social gospel' as a term of derision – a term with a wholly American provenance, significantly different from the genres of Christian social action in the UK, yet frequently used among conservatives here to denote a kind of faith practice with which they take issue. It suggests that some of the theological ammunition deployed in conflicts within the British churches is actually manufactured in the United States.

In contrast, the so-called theological liberals are (paradoxically, given the universalist aspirations of the liberal project) significantly less international in outlook. Perhaps the tendency of theological liberalism to underpin established church structures in Western Europe has left liberals wedded to a model of the nation state which is under challenge from globalization. Perhaps resistance to the global market reinforces a somewhat defensive localism. Nevertheless, just because theological liberals in Europe have been slow to explore their contemporary global relationships, it does not mean that models of church life from another continent can be straightforwardly adopted as panaceas for local ills.

But, whether through direct importing of models, networking exchanges, or sheer transatlantic envy, conservative American understandings of church life are finding Europe – especially Britain – to be fertile ground. And here another paradox surfaces – for the American churches are castigated both as the epitome of liberal waywardness and as the fountainhead of fundamentalist intolerance. Can both views be right?

Indeed they can. The profound individualism of the American models of liberal democracy and capitalist economics has generated a powerful identity politics, in which people define themselves as members of quite tightly defined interest groups, and this provokes strident tensions and conflicts. In other words, the competitiveness at the heart of market systems is highly stressful in terms of the human desire to belong and to maintain secure boundaries which protect identity. Inevitably the stresses emerge in profound disagreements about the ills of society.

Yet again, the limitations of the word 'liberal' come into play. When ECUSA is condemned for the election of Gene Robinson to the episcopate, the liberalism under attack is a kind of liberal theology which sits uncomfortably within the wider economic liberalism of American polity. And if we add up the conservatives who object to Robinson's appointment, they come largely from a wider American Christian movement, far broader and more extensive than Anglicanism, which thrives in the context of the liberal economic settlement that has shaped America. That American Christianity is often not only acquiescent in, but actively enthusiastic for, the US economic model with its stress on individualism and the virtue of wealth acquisition. In some ways ECUSA reflects the British dilemma about American market ideology – whether to resist or celebrate it. The two sides in the homosexuality debate represent, at one level, two Americas, both with a claim to stand for something particularly American. No wonder the debate appears to carry a great deal of freight. Major questions of national – and global – identity are in play here. But so too is a conflict between 'liberals' who privilege the virtue of social tolerance and the 'liberals' who celebrate economic freedom.

Therein may lie a partial explanation of liberalism's apparent inability (whether in theology, politics or economics) to give an adequate analysis of the ills that beset today's world. The liberal project has been neglectful of its own account of virtue – indeed, the whole tradition of the virtues is one which classic liberalism sought to usurp in favour of a universalist appeal to human reason. In practice, so-called liberals do have an ethic of the virtues – tolerance, plurality, freedom, non-violence and so on. But the tradition has been neglected to the extent that there is no agreement, and few mechanisms for agreeing, on a coherent account of how the liberal virtues can be lived.

The political psychology of being part of a global economy, dominated by particular norms, is complex but inescapable. As Orwell noted, the appeal of the powerful can make willing slaves of many. The genius of the current economic order is to create areas of social interaction where the identity politics of 'us' and 'them' can be practised without posing a major threat to the basic economic order. Thus far at least, dissent around issues of personal morality, especially sexual ethics, has been one such area of social space. As I will suggest, there are interesting questions about whether this will endure.

The role of religion in underpinning economic order is complex but more influential than most market apologists tend to allow. From R. H. Tawney in the 1920s onwards, it has been accepted that the particular emphases of Protestant theology have been factors in the growth of capitalist economics to their present position of global dominance (Tawney 1926). An interesting question for today is how far the rise of 'furious religion' (for example, fundamentalist Christianity, militant Islam or aggressive Zionism) is a reaction to the current phase of global economic development. In many ways it appears to constitute a renewed, if narrow, collectivism in response to the manifest weaknesses and failings of modernist individualism, including the economic individualism of market economics.

## Capitalism and being human

There is much evidence that the market has been a Leviathan before which innumerable social bonds and community virtues have been sacrificed. The sociologist Richard Sennett has exposed the problems of communicating moral virtues between the generations when the 'ethics' of the marketplace do so much to undermine or negate ideas such as trust, loyalty and truth-telling (Sennett 1998). Sennett has also noted how work and employment patterns in the West have generated a widespread sense of social uselessness among the workforce. A society of individuals, trained through market mechanisms to be suspicious of one another and to value competitiveness above solidarity or community, is conscious of what it has lost and yet has no vocabulary for identifying either the cause of its ills or the source of possible solutions without undermining the economic consensus which presents itself as the only salvation.

Francis Fukuyama was notoriously premature in his announcement of the end of history once the alternatives to market capitalism had apparently disappeared, but he was right to identify the prevailing belief that there is only one show left in town (Fukuyama 1992). Is it surprising, then, that any analysis of the profound social alienation of our times should baulk at solutions which appear to demolish the whole edifice of apparent prosperity and peace? Instead, the reaction to the bleakness of social fragmentation under contemporary market economics emerges in forms which allow cultural anxieties to be expressed. They generate a strong sense of belonging through the creation of impermeable social boundaries, yet remain uncritical or even supportive of the prevailing economic and political ideology that seems, almost literally, beyond question. Sennett identifies religion as a key beneficiary of this kind of social anxiety. The British economic commentator Will Hutton agrees that the rise of stridently defensive religion in America is, in part, such a reaction, and suggests that similar factors are seen in Europe more in the rise of nationalisms of various kinds (Hutton 2006). This may be true but it does not preclude the importation of elements of American religion into the British social context for similar reasons.

My suggestion here is that the strength of anti-gay attitudes in the religious world of today is not unconnected with the deep-felt need for people to find expressions of solidarity which do not implicate the all-embracing market ideology on which their survival appears to rest. In such a setting, there is a strong need to identify a threatening 'other' against which the uprightness and reliability of 'people like us' can be measured. This shadow side of identity politics becomes a kind of displacement activity taking the place of the hard, and risky, work of real community-building which could challenge the idea of prosperity crudely measured by market wealth. And this hunt for the 'other' is less an attack on individual gay and lesbian people than an expression of cultural dissent. What is not scrutinized is the umbilical link between the public manipulation of sexual imagery – including gay and lesbian imagery – and the marketization of culture generally. Safe dissent must focus on peripheral targets. But safe dissent is rather different from a prophetic vocation.

Somewhere in all this lies one basic difficulty at the heart of western political life – the market's rapacious tendency to destroy and devalue virtues such as community, mutuality and the common good which people both need and recognize they need. The unregulated tendency of markets is always towards monopoly, thus wherever markets are allowed free rein, practices which treat people as ends and not means are eroded as money becomes the only measurement of value which counts and as power tends to concentrate in fewer and fewer hands. Yet, economically, we ride the tiger – getting off seems riskier than staying put. It seems reasonable to suggest that enlisting religion as a political motif (stridently by Bush, tentatively by Blair) is an attempt to find a vocabulary of community, mutuality and solidarity that does not compromise an overall commitment to global market economics. This becomes easier when religious energies are channelled into issues (such as homosexuality) about who is 'in' and who is 'out' rather than fundamental questions of economic morality.

## A proxy issue?

As a small exercise illustrating that assertion, consider the two most strident denunciations of Christian leaders in Britain in the last twenty years. In the mid-1980s, David Jenkins, Bishop of Durham, was pilloried for his supposedly unorthodox views on the virgin birth and resurrection. No matter that what he said had been unexceptional in theology and in church life for decades. No matter that he never denied the resurrection but that his words were consistently misreported to imply that he had. (Constantly reported as saying that the resurrection was 'just a conjuring trick with bones', Jenkins had actually said that the resurrection must be *more* than just a conjuring trick.) Jenkins took the full opprobrium of the conservative press, the Conservative party and those sections of the Church which are most insistent that their truth represents orthodoxy. The virulence of the campaign so far outweighed Jenkins' religious significance (and was so blatantly based upon misreporting and stubborn misrepresentation) as to suggest that it was a proxy for some other issue which his detractors would not address directly.

Cut forward to the translation of Rowan Williams to Canterbury in 2002. Immediately his appointment was announced, the focus turned to his supposed views on homosexuality. No matter that his actual statements were framed within a profoundly theological world-view. No matter that he himself saw the issue as peripheral. The virulence of the campaign against Williams equalled that against Jenkins almost twenty years before, with the difference that this time there was 'collateral damage' in the person of Jeffrey John who became the personal embodiment of the case against Williams.

In both cases, the disproportionate stridency of the campaigns tended to obscure other stances that Jenkins and Williams had very publicly taken. The former was outspoken in his attacks on Margaret Thatcher's economic policies, most notably her destruction of the British coalfields and their communities. Williams has been a persistent campaigner against nuclear weaponry and a subtle critic of market economics and its effects. Both brought formidable intellectual and moral stature to their episcopal roles. Yet no head-on confrontation with these wider political stances was really attempted. Instead their supposed (or manufactured) doctrinal unorthodoxy became the focus of opposition within the churches, which served to weaken their wider political impact – for if they could not carry their Christian constituency with them, why should they command attention in the secular world?

I do not contend that those churchpeople who joined the clamour against Williams and Jenkins were consciously fighting a battle for the well-being of the market economy. But given the strange exaggeration of those bishops' doctrinal views and the power of their political theology and moral commentary on economics, the furore is suggestive. Marxists used to speak of 'useful idiots' – those who could be co-opted for their own reasons to join a cause that was of greater significance than they knew and subtly furthered the Party's interests. The ideologues of the market economy are generally neutral to questions of faith (and sexuality) but opponents like Jenkins and Williams, who are theologically sceptical of the market's claims and who potentially command the moral allegiances of significant constituencies, posed an 'objective threat' (to use another Marxist formula) which could not have been comfortable.

Indeed, the cases of Jenkins and Williams are reinforced by the recent attacks on John Gladwin, Bishop of Chelmsford, for his openness to dialogue with gay people. Gladwin is Chair of Christian Aid, an organization that has not been shy of critiquing the structures of the global market and, as a result, has sometimes had to fend off attacks from the political Right. Discrediting Gladwin as a Christian leader may be part of a tactic to weaken Christian Aid's undoubted ability to irritate the free marketeers.

My suggestion that sexuality has become a proxy issue, under whose cloak the critics of the market economy can be marginalized, is quite easily dismissed as fantasy if one accepts the conventional (but increasingly tired) view of secularization, which assumes the inevitable decline of religion in the West. Why should a couple of bishops warrant anyone's attention when no one significant believes in God anyway? But that version of secularization is much discredited and religion is now a major player in global politics. Taking religion seriously as a political force, it is hardly surprising that any dominant ideology will expend considerable energy to neutralize religious dissent by steering it towards internal church questions of marginal economic significance. Perhaps the gay issue in the churches is not so much a matter of liberals versus conservatives as a clash between the political Left and the political Right.

## Market trends, gay people and Africa

But are gay people really marginal to the market? Here, I think, we are about to witness some interesting developments and I hesitate to predict their trajectory. If I am right to suggest that it is the spending power of gay people which has, in part, allowed them to take a more prominent role in a market-dominated culture, then it may be that a fervent anti-gay stance among religions could become a problem for the economy. My suspicion is that the gay market is, so far, just large enough to be worth exploiting but not yet really mainstream. It could become so; in which case, watch out for the gradual marginalization of anti-gay movements, whether religious or secular. The openness to gay people emerging in Conservative social policy under David Cameron is interesting in this regard. But capitalism is, of its nature, protean. Conspiracy theories are of only limited value in predicting its trends (which is not to say that there are no pro-capitalist conspiracies). If anti-gay sentiments were to harden significantly and spread, driven perhaps by rising global anger at the market's hegemony, the market's self-protective mechanisms might respond by reflecting this rather than countering it. It all depends which response is economically preferable. That is one implication of a system which is avowedly unconstrained by religious or moral narratives and neutral concerning the moral claims of discrete communities. The paradox is that relying on market forces to liberalize social attitudes makes the gay community beholden to the very ideology which diminishes and undermines concepts of community and the virtues – concepts that many thoughtful gay people understand to be essential for their flourishing.

And this brings us back to Africa – and all the peoples who have been impoverished and marginalized by the global market. Is Africa's economic future within or outside the market consensus? If western cultural dissent has been channelled away from a critique of economics for fear of the prosperity vacuum which weakening the market might imply, such constraints hardly apply to those who have never felt significant benefits from the global market. I am no expert on Africa or the African Church, but I can well imagine that, from an African perspective, the connection between homosexual visibility and a marketized consumer society looks entirely obvious, the one seen as part and parcel of the other. This is not to justify the anti-gay attitudes of some African churches, but to recognize that the subtleties of the arguments familiar in the West, which try to distinguish the liberalism of sexual tolerance from the liberalism of market economics, say little to the African context. It remains that Africa – and the African churches – have to work out a relationship to new global market structures, especially the dominant 'Washington' economic model. Whether Africa's economic future lies in an attempt to reform the Washington model, or whether a more confrontational stance offers any more hope, is a question well beyond the scope of this essay. Suffice to say that the well-documented global alliances of anti-gay Christians may hang together less easily as the African economy rises up the list of international – and church – priorities.

# An agenda for theology

I am not suggesting that the more overtly theological questions surrounding the sexuality debate are negligible. On the contrary, questions such as the use of the Bible, the development of Christian moral understandings and the way Christians use evidence from supposedly secular disciplines are all crucial to the perplexities of Christian living today. Some of those points are discussed elsewhere in this book. I am arguing that economic issues need to be given greater attention when we look at how Christians and churches actually behave. There is an agenda here for theological enquiry, which is pressing if the ramifications of the sexuality debate are to contribute to the churches' collective discipleship today. It is when we examine what Christian faith has to say about godly living in a global market economy that some of these questions become extremely stark.

Despite the real incoherence about the terms conservative and liberal, we still need such concepts to explore the relationship of Christian theology to the conflicting 'major narratives' of the global economy on the one hand and the human imperatives of community, relationship and identity on the other. Until the theological liberals find a way of expressing their concern for human solidarities in terms which do not contradict their espousal of the virtues of freedom, conscience and toleration, they will find it impossible to pose any viable challenge to the market's attenuated image of being human. It may be that the shared roots of the theological liberals and the economic liberals are too close and that the liberal theological project is thus a dead end in terms of critiquing the way we live now. But I believe there remain some avenues worth exploring.

For those who eschew the liberal project and focus instead on Christian identity, community and counter-cultural living, the great lacuna at present is a coherent account of living in economic terms. The few Christian communities, like the Amish, which have tried to live outside the dominant market consensus have found it hard to do so without significant compromises. Nevertheless, the compromises do not completely invalidate the attempt. Contemporary theologies which, similarly, focus on the distinctive nature and practices of the Christian community (such as the work of Stanley Hauerwas) offer a sexual ethic which focuses on the theological themes of fidelity and respect for creation rather than differentiating between gay and straight practices. In my view, this is a more authentic 'orthodoxy' than the commonly argued anti-gay position, and it is often at odds with mainstream American views about, for example, militarism, and out of line with much conservative religious opinion. There remains the criticism that this form of counter-cultural living relies covertly on the tolerance inherent in liberal democracy. It would be enlightening to explore the translation of Hauerwasian theology to the context of, say, Nigeria, and see how such themes worked out there. At any rate, it is clear that counter-culturalism is a major force in contemporary Christian ethics, but in ways which certainly do not make sexuality the touchstone of Christian orthodoxy (Hauerwas 2001). Unless and until the contradictions of espousing the market economy and simultaneously seeking to mark out Christian orthodoxy on grounds of sexuality are faced, the so-called conservative position will be vulnerable to the charge that it is essentially more interested in bolstering the political Right than in theological and ethical problems.

The picture is no more reassuring for the liberals. The present marginalization of the liberal theological tradition within the churches and the academy is, to a large extent, self-inflicted. The end of consensus and political optimism in the mid-1970s was met with heroic resistance in the churches on behalf of the poor and marginalized, but with little serious theology, and almost none which explored the connections between the liberal virtues and the market's ill effects.

Theological liberalism seems to have gone from hubris to insignificance in one step, but that does not make it a mere aberration or wrong turning. The next step is surely to recover an authentic theological narrative about where the liberal virtues of tolerance, conscience and so on figure in classic Christian vocabulary. Christian orthodoxy, rightly, holds in tension (but does not fully synthesize) the idea of the kingdom inaugurated with the idea of the kingdom not yet fully realized. It is this concept of the theological interim, between Pentecost and the end of all things, that creates space for liberal virtues to be understood as being among the theological virtues. That in turn leads to an informed distancing of theological liberalism from the all-embracing ambitions of the liberal market project – not least, because of the potential for a theological account of human freedom and human community which holds both in tension without privileging a narrow, utilitarian account of virtue. It is significant that 'liberal' theologians as different as Ronald Preston (on the political Left) and Michael Novak (on the Right) have retained a concern for communitarian values as a corrective to liberal universalism. The tragedy is that communitarian and confessional theologians have rarely distinguished the theological virtues of liberalism from liberalism's political and economic manifestations.

The controversy about homosexuality has exposed another weakness in both liberal and conservative theologies: the lack of a coherent public theology. In this, conservatives perhaps have the advantage as their concern for the right conduct of Christians is addressed to the churches and diminishes any need to make theology intelligible in the public square. Nevertheless, conservative Christians rarely confine their strictures to their own members. 'Liberals', who once saw public theology as integral to their faith, lost confidence in that project once the marginalization of the churches in public life became inescapable. It remains that Christians' public stances towards the global economy are a pressing matter for liberals and conservatives alike if they seek an authentic discipleship. Their answers may be different, but the churches badly need some theology of engagement with the public sphere of politics and economics.

## Conclusion

Today's Church exists, whether it likes it or not, in a context and a culture moulded largely by the demands of the market economy. Yet what goes on in the City of London, and the other great engine rooms of the market, is strangely absent from many Christian expressions of moral concern. It is not that economic questions trump issues of sexual morality but that examining one without the other is incoherent. A consideration of economic power and market trends helps us locate the debate about homosexuality within a bigger argument in which the Church is only one player. Factoring in the economic dimension goes a little way towards helping us differentiate the position of conservative African Christians from that of their fellow conservatives in the West. Most of all, I am convinced that questions of economics expose the inadequacy of much contemporary Christian ethics – and that when those gaps are filled, we stand a chance of seeing the sexuality debate in rather clearer terms.

## References

Davie, G., *Europe: The Exceptional Case*, Darton, Longman & Todd, London, 2002.

Fukuyama, F., *The End of History and the Last Man*, Penguin, Harmondsworth, 1992.

Hauerwas, S., 'Why gays (as a group) are morally superior to Christians (as a group)' in J. Berkman and M. Cartwright (eds), *The Hauerwas Reader,* Duke University Press, Durham and London, 2001, pp. 519–21.

Hutton, W., 'You're 35 and experienced. Let's face it, you're useless', *Observer*, 12 March 2006.

Richter, P. and Francis, L., *Gone but not Forgotten: Church Leaving and Returning*, Darton, Longman & Todd, London, 1998.

Sennett, R., *The Corrosion of Character*, W. W. Norton, New York, 1998.

Tawney, R. H., *Religion and the Rise of Capitalism*, Penguin, Harmondsworth, 1926 and subsequent editions.

# 11

# HIV/AIDS: the real challenge for the Anglican Communion?

MICHAEL BEASLEY

The conflict concerning different attitudes to homosexuality is developing a fault line within the Anglican Communion. To one side of this line lie those who believe that homosexuality is a lifestyle that is consciously chosen by some in contravention of natural norms. To the other side of the line are those who believe that it is not valid to think that those who are homosexual have any real choice in the matter; by nature and nurture they are who they are. Put another way, some in the Communion consider that those who are homosexual are choosing to be sinful while others believe that homosexuals are living in the way they have been created. To a large extent these differences in opinion reflect the Communion's cultural diversity that includes a (usually) more liberal North and a (usually) more conservative South. However, rather than recognizing that the issue is primarily cultural each side chooses to argue for the ascendancy of its own position, cherry-picking moral, ethical and scriptural evidence to back their belief that their own world-view is the correct one.

It would be bad enough if the situation outlined were to result in those in the Communion of one viewpoint choosing to separate themselves from those of the other. But for millions, the impact of the fault line that has developed is much graver. For the schism that is developing within the Communion is fundamentally damaging its ability to respond effectively to the most important issue in human sexuality facing the world today, the HIV/AIDS pandemic that affects around 40 million people, many of whom will die as a result of their infection. Mounting an effective response to HIV/AIDS demands global attention and an almost unprecedented partnership of skills and perspectives including the theological, logistical, financial and technical. As a worldwide organization, the Anglican Communion is extremely well placed to bring together many of the different resources that are required to address the pandemic. The fault line that is developing between different parts of the Communion threatens to jeopardize this ability in several ways. First, it acts to distract attention from a highly pressing situation. HIV/AIDS poses some difficult questions for the church community, particularly in the area of stigma and discrimination to which religious thought has contributed so much. Adequately addressing these questions demands enormous care and attention that can too often be sidelined as the conflict about homosexuality takes centre stage. Second, the fault line damages the ability of the Communion to work together for good, divorcing the different contributions that different parts of the Communion can make towards prevention and mitigation of the disease. At its most simplistic this means separating those on the ground in a position to help the people affected (southern Christians) from those who have the financial and political clout adequately to respond to the scale of the pandemic (northern Christians).

## A global pandemic

In 2005, it was estimated that 40.3 million people in the world were living with the infection. Of these, 17.5 million are women (the fastest growing group among those affected by the pandemic). In addition, it is also estimated that around 2.3 million children under 15 years are infected. And the pandemic continues to grow: last year 4.9 million people were newly infected with HIV and 3.1 million died of AIDS.

Although HIV is found in all other parts of the world and is showing worrying signs of increase, especially in Asia and Eastern Europe, over half of all infections are found in sub-Saharan Africa where around 26 million people are now thought to be living with the infection (UNAIDS 2005).

Inevitably, millions of children have been orphaned or made vulnerable by HIV/AIDS. In sub-Saharan Africa alone, an estimated 12.3 million children are now without their parents (UNAIDS *et al.* 2004). This number is set to rise over the next decade as HIV-positive parents become ill and die from their infection. Obviously, the rise in orphans is of enormous concern both to the individuals themselves, but also for the long-term welfare and sustainability of the countries in which they live.

## An issue affecting entire nations

HIV/AIDS is a personal and particular catastrophe affecting millions of people around the world. It also presents a long-term development issue affecting the fate of whole countries, economies and cultures. The infection has the capacity to destroy whole sectors of countries' economies and to reverse precious development gains made during the last twenty years. For example, in Zambia, it was estimated that 2 per cent of the country's teachers died of AIDS in the year 2001. The experience of such loss over a number of years has presented the country with severe challenges, undermining its ability to staff its schools and to fulfil its goal of providing all Zambian children with a primary school education by the year 2015.

Education is just one sector of the country's economy. HIV/AIDS is having similar disastrous consequences in all other parts of the lives of nations: transport, health care, agriculture and so on. The disease acts only to exacerbate Africa's underdevelopment and instability, severely limiting its ability to overcome the problems that have dogged the continent over past decades.

## A sexually transmitted infection

The overwhelming majority of cases of HIV/AIDS found in the world have been transmitted through heterosexual sexual contact. Other much less common causes of transmission include (in rough order of import-ance) mother–to–child transmission (the cause of most infections among children aged less than 15 years), entry of infected blood into the body (through contaminated blood transfusions and sharing of needles among intravenous drug users) and homosexual sexual contact.

In most people, around ten years elapses between infection with the human immunodeficiency virus (HIV) and the onset of symptomatic illness – Acquired Immune Deficiency Syndrome (AIDS). This 'hidden' character of the infection has contributed much to the ability of the virus to be widely transmitted through populations, unlike other sexu-ally transmitted diseases which tend to be much more apparent and which are usually restricted to those engaged in 'high–risk' behaviours such as promiscuous homosexual sexual activity or prostitution. In the case of HIV a youthful sexual encounter years ago can lead to the infection of a faithful partner years later.

There is no cure for HIV/AIDS. In recent years, drugs that control the symptoms of HIV infection, called anti–retrovirals (also called ARVs or ART), have become increasingly available at low cost. But prescription and distribution of these drugs is highly complex, placing additional strain on health services that are themselves being destroyed by the infection. ARVs are by no means benign and may have highly unpleasant side–effects.

## The Christian churches and HIV/AIDS

HIV/AIDS is a crisis facing the whole of humanity and as such demands the attention and action of Christian churches. Churches' responses to the epidemic have varied significantly. On the one hand, some churches have addressed the situation with pastoral and moral sensitivity and play a highly significant role in the mitigation and prevention of the disease. Other churches have addressed the situation in ways that lead to the condemnation, stigmatization and discrimination of those affected. Such stigmatization is highly damaging to efforts to control infection. For where infection is thought to affect only 'bad people' societies tend not to take the urgent actions needed to bring the disease under control. Matters are made worse as those affected fail to come forward for testing and treatment. In turn many fail to change their behaviour to prevent the infection of others and do not access care and support provided by HIV and AIDS services.

At the heart of churches' tensions in responding to HIV/AIDS is the uncomfortable fact that the disease is a sexually transmitted infection that results in mortality. As such it touches on two of humanity's greatest 'taboo' subjects – sex and death. HIV/AIDS is one of the very few diseases where our response to hearing that a person is affected is to ask, 'How did this person become infected?' Too often, this reality acts to transform a pastoral and medical question (How can this person be helped?) into a question of moral judgement (Why did this person behave in the way they did to become infected?). Having made such a move, a subsequent response is often to seek to apportion blame for the situation. Blame responses tend to be polarized between those that apportion responsibility to individuals and those that point at the structures of society. The former is all too familiar from the early days of the epidemic when HIV was spoken of as a 'gay plague', a divine response meted out to those living 'wicked' lifestyles. The latter response, of blaming the structures of society has occurred more as the factors driving the epidemic, particularly in sub-Saharan Africa, have become better understood. Ignorance, malnutrition, gender inequity and other factors related to poverty are all now known to foster the transmission of infection. This has led some, like the organization Christian Aid, to argue that 'If covenantal relationships between God and his people, and by extension, between those people themselves, are to be restored and maintained, the various forms of injustice that underlie the spread of HIV have to be addressed' (Clifford 2004, p. 1).

There is of course truth in both of these tendencies, but their polarization leads to a distorted picture of reality. So, for example, the young girl who chooses to have sex with a stranger in order that she might eat that day is hardly acting out of individual wickedness; she is driven to extreme action by the situation of poverty in which she lives. Entirely the opposite is to be said of the rich businessman who offers the girl a meal for sex.

# Living positively

The problem, of course, with responding to HIV/AIDS through the medium of blame and recrimination is that very little is ever achieved by such recourse. Individuals who are the subject of blame so often turn a deaf ear. With respect to the societal causes of the disease, while campaigning about single, simple issues is sometimes effective, campaigning about the highly complex and multifaceted issues that contribute to the environment in which HIV flourishes is much more difficult. When the dominant response is to blame, the fundamental pastoral question posed by HIV/AIDS, 'How can this person be helped?' goes unanswered.

At a very practical level, a much more effective response to the situation has been developed by people living with HIV/AIDS themselves through the philosophy of 'living positively', an idea that was taken up and promoted by 'The AIDS Support Organisation' (TASO) of Uganda and subsequently widely adopted throughout the world (Kaleeba 2002). The programme seeks to address everyone in society, both those infected with HIV and those who are uninfected. It calls on those who are HIV-positive to live responsibly with their infection, and to ensure that they do not pass it on to others. It also calls upon those who are infected to take care of themselves and to remain actively involved in society. But 'living positively' also calls upon the rest of society to support and accept people living with HIV/AIDS and not to stigmatize or discriminate against them. A critical component of the approach is the encouragement to all people to know their HIV status, either positive or negative: 'You can't begin living positively if you do not know that you are HIV-positive.'

## From practice to theology

Fundamental to the concept of 'living positively' is the acceptance of a person's HIV status, both by the person affected and by those living with them. Such acceptance frees those living with HIV/AIDS from the snares of wishing that HIV/AIDS did not exist or that it does not affect them. It enables those affected to accept themselves and others as they are, rather than the people they would like to be. Those who 'live positively' are enabled therefore to recognize themselves as people both with sexual histories (which may be more or less ideal) and, critically, as people with a future. They are not exclusively defined by what has gone before and therefore are open to change and hope, to memory and lament.

Speaking of infection, Louis Pasteur once said, 'the virus is nothing, the terrain is everything'. This is to say that the transmission or prevention of infection depends not so much upon the capabilities of a virus

147

as on the favourability of the environmental conditions in which it seeks to spread. From both a theological and epidemiological perspective, the terrain in which the HIV virus flourishes is the human condition itself. In scripture, the part of the Bible that has addressed the human condition at its thorniest and most fundamental is probably St Paul's letter to the Romans. In the first chapter, Paul tackles the 'environment' of the human condition head-on. He argues that no human life is ideal, that no one lives a life that is perfect. Furthermore, Paul diagnoses the root of the 'problem' with being human as the attempt to put us, and our experience, at the centre of the universe rather than God. By failing to honour God, and in consequence failing to live fully in accordance with the will of God, Paul claims that human lives are fundamentally disordered: 'For though they knew God, they did not honour him as God or give thanks to him, but they became futile in their thinking and their senseless minds were darkened' (Romans 1:21).

Paul argues that because human beings fail to honour God, to put him at the centre of their lives, human beings are in consequence left to their own devices, left prey to their passing desires, whims and passions. Paul posits that this has the disastrous consequence of sins, dysfunction and misery that affect so much of humankind so much of the time: 'Therefore God gave them up in the lusts of their hearts to impurity, to the degrading of their bodies among themselves, because they exchanged the truth about God for a lie and worshipped and served the creature rather than the Creator' (Romans 1.24–5).

Paul's diagnosis presents a compelling perspective on what is happening with the HIV/AIDS pandemic. Humankind's failure to honour the Creator establishes through a complex interplay of individual and social forces a terrain conducive to the transmission of the disease. At the level of the individual, transmission occurs because, at some point, someone in a person's network of contacts has chosen to enact a behaviour that has been risky. At a social level, populations have chosen to pursue policies that lead to the widespread poverty, ignorance, gender inequity and vulnerability in which the transmission of the virus thrives. (An example of this is the decision of the EU and the USA to subsidize the work of their agricultural sectors. This gives western farmers unfair advantage that leads to the impoverishment of millions in the less developed world.) All these factors, both individual and social, are a result of humankind's inability to honour and live in accordance with the will of the Creator. It is this inability that forms the basis for theological reflection on HIV/AIDS and the environment of its transmission.

Paul is adamant that the situation he describes pertains to every human being. Everyone has fallen short of God's will for their life in their own particular way. By extension, all of us, either through our individual actions or by complicity in inequitable global political systems, bear some level of responsibility for the global pandemic that is causing the untimely death of millions. All then, be they northern or southern Christians, HIV-positive or not, gay or straight, stand equally condemned under the just judgement of a righteous God.

A key aspect of 'living positively' is the call upon society to support and accept people living with HIV/AIDS and not to stigmatize or discriminate against them. Paul's argument goes far beyond this. In Romans he makes the claim that self-righteous judgement of any behaviour is as bad as the behaviour itself:

> You say, 'We know that God's judgement on those who do such things is in accordance with the truth.' Do you imagine, whoever you are, that when you judge those who do such things and yet do them yourself, you will escape the judgement of God? (Romans 2.2–3)

Those who stigmatize and condemn the presumed behaviour of those who have had the misfortune to become HIV-positive are guilty of sins quite the equal of those they imagine the infected to have undertaken. In Paul's theology there is no room for blame, stigmatization, or the creation of scapegoats. With respect to HIV/AIDS we need to recognize that the infection is an unfortunate consequence of the fallenness of the world in which all of us live.

Paul's diagnosis extends far beyond mere description of our human condition. In his letter he continues to offer to humankind his understanding of the solution to our problems. Paul makes the claim that through faith, salvation is offered to all people, no matter what has gone before. Paul's gospel is good news for all of us, whether we are HIV-positive or HIV-negative, whether we have personally engaged in risky behaviour that has led to HIV transmission or been complicit in social systems that fuel the spread of the disease; whether we are the faithful housewife infected as a consequence of a husband's youthful sexual encounter or the pension fund member whose investments have destroyed a developing world market in pursuit of higher dividends: 'God proves his love for us in that while we still were sinners Christ died for us. If while we were enemies, we were reconciled to God through the death of his Son, much more surely, having been reconciled, will we be saved by his life' (Romans 5.8, 10).

In summary, the practical consequences of Pauline theology for HIV/AIDS are:

- All human beings, through our inability to honour God live lives marred by sin. All then are implicated in establishing the 'terrain' in which HIV can flourish.

- Self-righteous judgement of those affected by the consequences of sin, including HIV/AIDS, is the equal of the behaviour being condemned. There is thus no room whatsoever for stigmatization or condemnation of those affected by the infection.
- The ultimate hope for all people, both HIV-positive and HIV-negative is the salvation of Jesus Christ. This depends on faith, not upon who we are or what we have done.

# From theology to practice

The concept of 'living positively' is in accord both with the lived experience of people living with HIV/AIDS and with the fundamental principles of the gospel. As such, it can help focus the practice of Christians towards the areas where they can achieve maximum impact: challenging the stigma that so often surrounds HIV/AIDS, care of those affected by the infection and prevention of its transmission.

## Challenging stigma

As has already been mentioned, religious beliefs can contribute to stigma by considering HIV as punishment from God for living an immoral lifestyle. A report based on conversations with people living with HIV/AIDS in Ethiopia, Tanzania and Zambia found the following typical statements among respondents:

'They relate HIV with evil. They say it came from God.' (Ethiopia)
'So they say if you got it then you are like Satan.' (Tanzania)
'[We] consider the sick to be more sinners than Satan.' (Zambia)
(International Centre for Research on Women 2003)

Disentangling the causes of such a response is a complex activity. Stigma arises from a wide range of causes including fear, prejudice, ignorance and inadequacy. When a community feels threatened in this way from within, a common response is to find a surrogate victim who becomes the focus of blame. Such scapegoating of an individual or a group has a cathartic effect with their removal or ostracization, leaving the community feeling purified and at peace. HIV flourishes in some of the harshest and most difficult places in the world and those affected can place great demands upon individuals and communities charged with their care. While it may be deeply unfortunate, it is quite understandable that those affected with HIV/AIDS are identified as scapegoats by individuals whose lives are a continual round of threat, anxiety and instability.

Stigma is also the product of our inability to accept parts of our lives with which we cannot deal and are perhaps ashamed. A common response in countries heavily affected by the infection is to suppose that strict adherence to religious strictures will ward off the disease:

> This disease is the result of our sin and our distance from religion. If we didn't commit sin this thing would never have come. Thus God will be merciful for us if we get closer to our religion. If we do good things and obey God's law, there will be no disease that has no cure.
> (Ethiopia; International Centre for Research on Women 2003)

Such a response attempts to link HIV/AIDS exclusively to a single person's actions rather than recognize that the disease, driven by both individual and social determinants, is more symptomatic of the fallenness with which all humankind is implicated.

Finally, stigma arises when people are faced with things they cannot control and which evoke the feeling of fear. The least controllable thing in life is death. For millions in the world that inevitability occurs prematurely through the impact of HIV/AIDS. It is hardly surprising if it results in stigma.

Churches, in common with many different organizations, can do much to combat stigma. Common responses include interventions such as:

- creation of greater recognition of stigma and discrimination
- fostering of in-depth, applied knowledge of HIV/AIDS
- provision of safe spaces to discuss values and beliefs about sex, morality and death
- promotion of common language to talk about stigma
- ensuring central, appropriate and responsible roles for people with HIV/AIDS.

In addition to these common responses, churches have a unique responsibility to tackle a fundamental *religious* cause of stigmatization of those affected by HIV/AIDS: the reduction of religion to some kind of behavioural tick list. Rather, there is a need constantly to restate the facts that 'since all have sinned and fall short of the glory of God; they are now justified by his grace as a gift' (Romans 3.23–24). Such an understanding underpins the philosophy of 'living positively' and enables society to support and accept people living with HIV/AIDS. For it sees them not just as 'sinners' to be condemned but also as 'new creations' with whom to be reconciled.

## Care and prevention

Freeing people from the tendency to stigmatize and discriminate against those affected by HIV/AIDS enables them to respond to the pandemic in creative and effective ways. In the less developed world, the concept of 'state social services' as understood in more prosperous countries is barely developed. In such countries, the contribution of faith-based organizations is critical to the provision of care. In some countries of sub-Saharan Africa, for example, it has been estimated that around one-third of the health and education infrastructure is provided by faith-based organizations (Foster 2004).

In Africa, not only do faith-based organizations provide infrastructure, their reach extends to almost all the continent's population. More than 99.5 per cent of Africa's 750 million people have a religious allegiance and more than 2 million congregations blanket the continent. The majority of faith-based organizations have initiatives that care for those affected by HIV/AIDS, particularly the continent's 12.3 million orphans. Initiatives are proliferating and cover a wide range of different responses and are able to mobilize large numbers of volunteers. While the activities of congregations or religious co-ordinating bodies (such as dioceses or circuits) may be small, their enormous number means that their capacity to reach out at a scale much wider than governmental or non-governmental efforts is considerable. For example, in six sub-Saharan African countries, 360 faith-based organizations surveyed during a study supported a total of 156,754 orphans and vulnerable children. In a country such as Kenya, which is estimated to have 75,000 faith-based congregations, the potential for widespread care of those affected by HIV/AIDS is clearly of enormous magnitude (Foster 2004).

There is increasing evidence that linking care of those affected with HIV/AIDS to efforts to prevent transmission enhances the impact, sustainability, visibility and credibility of the latter (International HIV/AIDS Alliance 2000). Practical strategies that act effectively to link care and prevention include:

- participation of people living with HIV/AIDS in the delivery of care and support. Contact and experience of those infected with the virus can have a dramatic effect on behaviour change;
- provision of voluntary testing and counselling, and the emerging provision of ARV for HIV infection reinforces both prevention and care and support efforts enabling both behaviour change, and where necessary the appropriate management of opportunistic infections associated with the infection. In the case of pregnant women, the intervention can lead to a reduction in mother-to-child transmission and identification of care and support for mother and child.

An example of the way that care acts to support prevention efforts comes from Cambodia where community leaders involved in a joint Ministry of Health and NGO home-care initiative said: 'Until the home care teams started visiting, people didn't believe that there was AIDS in the village.' During an evaluation of the programme, 87 per cent of community leaders specifically said that the home care teams were helping to increase understanding of preventive measures. In Zambia, one HIV/AIDS programme member said: 'Programmes would not be complete without the combination of prevention and care. It's not meaningful if you do prevention without care, or care without prevention. The elements are inter-related and can't be separated. They're both integral to an effective programme' (International HIV/AIDS Alliance 2000, p. 7).

Provision of the care and prevention activities that has been described here demands the presence of both human and financial resources. Many Christians in areas severely affected by HIV/AIDS are doing their best to meet the needs of those worst affected. In practice this means that it is the 'faithful poor' who are helping the destitute. There is an urgent need for those reaching out to people affected by HIV/AIDS on the ground to receive the help and support of much more financially and politically powerful Christians around the world. Such work is undertaken by many different people, organizations and provinces of the Anglican Communion who provide both financial backing and who are well placed to lobby influential bodies such as governments, trade organizations and donors.

However, such life-saving initiatives are under threat as the Anglican Communion threatens to tear itself apart over questions of homosexuality. This threat was made quite explicit by the Archbishop of Nigeria, Peter Akinola, at a meeting of African Primates held in Nairobi in 2004: 'A few provinces have been receiving money for HIV/AIDS programmes and rehabilitation projects . . . If we denounce ECUSA, then it is also best that we refuse their money. We will not accept their money because they have decided to redefine Christianity to suit their needs' (Mulama 2006). Thus the ability of the Communion to work together for good is severely hampered.

## Conclusion

In recent years, the Anglican Communion has been much exercised in debate and discussion about a number of issues in human sexuality. However, the scale of the challenge posed by HIV/AIDS demands that the Communion shift its emphasis. The most pressing sexually related problem facing the Communion, and intimately affecting millions of its members, is not the question of homosexuality, it is the seemingly unstoppable HIV/AIDS pandemic, which is causing millions of Anglicans and others to die, millions of children to be made orphans, and whole countries and nations to be destabilized plunging them into ever-increasing poverty and turmoil.

While the first manifestations of HIV/AIDS occurred mainly among homosexual men, the infection is now firmly established as a disease affecting heterosexuals and increasingly a disease principally affecting women. Because of its long incubation period, transmission of the disease can affect perfectly ordinary people living lives that are no more risky or immoral than others. This reality should force Christians to consider the pandemic in the light of the human condition of the fallenness that affects us all.

Seeing HIV/AIDS as an ill for which we all bear some level of responsibility, either individually through our immediate actions or socially through our contribution to world systems that leave populations poor, ignorant and vulnerable, enables us to turn from the stigmatizaton and discrimination of those affected which so acts to fuel the spread of the infection. Taking responsibility for HIV/AIDS encourages *metanoia*, conversion, from viewing the infections negatively as 'someone else's problem' to the concept of 'living positively' in which all, both HIV-positive and HIV-negative, have their part to play in the fight against this evil.

Central to churches' efforts to address the issue of HIV/AIDS is the urgent need to reiterate the fundamental principles of the Christian gospel. Too often in practice, religious belief is reduced to a behavioural tick list, leaving those affected isolated, stigmatized and liable to behave in ways that will act only to fuel the infection's transmission. Christian concepts of grace, acceptance, new beginnings and new creation need to be asserted over such an impoverished view of faith and its dire consequences.

Evidence from sub-Saharan Africa shows that when churches and church members make such strides their impact can be phenomenal, playing a highly significant role in complementing the capacity of governmental and non-governmental organizations in severely affected countries. Not only can such activity act to care and support some of the world's most vulnerable people, it is also demonstrated to have the most significant impact in preventing the disease that is the cause of so much misery and anguish (International HIV/AIDS Alliance 2000).

Faith-based organizations, including those of the Anglican Communion, have enormous potential to act effectively to prevent and mitigate the impact of one of the most lethal evils the world has ever seen. Yet, the ability of the Communion to mount an effective response to HIV/AIDS has been put in jeopardy by its conflict over homosexuality. Those who have pressed their views so fiercely and raised the stakes have helped to impair the ability of different parts of the Communion to work together in addressing the issue. As Anglicans consider their response to issues in human sexuality it should be a matter of shame that such disunity over one issue, homosexuality, is sidelining attention from a pandemic that is causing the death, sorrow and suffering of millions.

# References

Clifford, P., 'Theology and the HIV/AIDS epidemic', Christian Aid, 2004. Available at http://www.e-alliance.ch/media/media-5348. Accessed 25.04.2006.

Foster, G., *Study of the Response by Faith-Based Organizations to Orphans and Vulnerable Children*, World Conference of Religions for Peace, UNICEF, 2004.

International Centre for Research on Women, *Disentangling HIV and AIDS Stigma in Ethiopia, Tanzania and Zambia*, ICRW, Washington DC, 2003. Available at http://www.icrw.org/docs/stigmareport093003.pdf. Accessed 25.04.2006.

International HIV/AIDS Alliance, *Care, Involvement and Action: Mobilising and supporting community responses to HIV/AIDS care and support in developing countries*, International HIV/AIDS Alliance, London, 2000.

Kaleeba, N., *We Miss You All: Noerine Kaleeba – AIDS in the Family*, SAfAIDS, Harare, 2002.

Mulama, J., 'Africa rejects donations from churches that support gay unions', *IPS News*, 16 April 2006. Available at http://www.ipsnews.net/interna.asp?idnews=23351. Accessed 25.04.2006.

UNAIDS (the joint United Nations Programme on HIV/AIDS), *AIDS Epidemic Update, December 2005*. Available at http://www.unaids.org/epi/2005/doc/report_pdf.asp. Accessed 25.04.2006.

UNAIDS, UNICEF and USAID, *Children on the Brink 2004: A joint report of new orphan estimates and a framework for action*, USAID, 2004.

# 12

# Selling body and soul in the 'fantasy economy'

DUNCAN DORMOR

In every age, the Church needs to pay serious attention to the world around it, to engage with what is happening and strive for some sense of proportion in its priorities and in the energy it devotes to certain discussions. As a contributor to a book on same-sex relationships I clearly believe the issue is of some importance. However, the issue remains one of *some* importance only – even within the arena of discussions about sexual ethics. Far more significant for the Church's missionary engagement with the world is the degree to which an unholy alliance has grown up, especially in the last decade, between the forces of consumerism and sexual gratification. This alliance promotes a distorted view of sexual desire and personhood: rather than enhancing the dignity and uniqueness of human individuals made in the image of God, sexual consumerism is increasingly moulding desires and bodies with powerful and distorting consequences for personal relationships and the common good. In the light of this rapid cultural shift, Christians who oppose the introduction of services of public commitment and blessing for same-sex relationships which are faithful, permanent and exclusive may have much more in common with their 'opponents' than they might imagine.

## Selling sex

Selling sex is hardly new. Prostitution is after all the 'oldest profession' in the world. What is new is the degree and diversity of ways in which human sexual desire is being manipulated and exploited for commercial profit; the pervasiveness and accessibility to the sexual services, products and practices that result; and the processes by which it is increasingly perceived to be legitimate within mainstream 'Western' culture. It is extremely difficult to provide reliable estimates for the 'value' of the 'adult entertainment industry' (hard-core videos and DVDs, Internet porn, cable and satellite porn, peep shows, phone sex, live sex acts, sexual toys and sex magazines). Nevertheless, for the US market, suggestions range from a conservative $3–4 billion to $8–10 billion dollars (Ackman 2001; Schlosser 2003) – the latter an amount equivalent to Hollywood's annual domestic box-office receipts.

Perhaps more significant than such bald statistics, or even the fact that this is an area of rapid economic expansion, is the realization that such activities are fully integrated with the emerging processes of globalization. Such processes allow for the greater fluidity and flow of people, products and services across time and space. So, for example, cheap and easy flights fuel the expansion of all that might broadly be described as sex tourism, just as the demand for cyber-sex and Internet pornography is driving the evolution of Web-based technologies.

Furthermore, there is a growing 'crossover' between mainstream society and the previously hidden world of the adult entertainment industry. In short, our culture is being heavily 'sexualized': 'Anonymous sexual encounters, once marked as the defining feature of prostitution, begin to be offered as entertainment and celebrated as the essence of a successful leisure experience' (Hawkes 2004, p. 7). Growth in the size and diversity of the commercial sex industry both stimulates and benefits from a more general shift in behaviour in which anonymous sexual encounters have become increasingly common and more acceptable. Boundaries are progressively eroded as 'adult entertainment' and mainstream culture converge. One emerging hotspot for such a 'sexualization' of culture is the international nightclub scene. Over 17 million young Britons (aged 16–34) travel abroad each year on holiday and increasing numbers choose such a destination. The possibilities for sexual adventure and activity are an integral part of both the marketing and the culture of such holidays. One recent study, which focused on Ibiza, found that on average such holiday-makers accumulated as many sexual partners in ten days as in the previous six months before their visit (Bellis *et al.* 2004).

Such a blurring of boundaries can be found in other places too: for example, in the world of medicine where initiatives originally with a clear therapeutic character are being developed and marketed to enhance sexual experience. The development of libido-enhancing drugs, most notably Viagra, for male sexual dysfunction has generated a climate in which allegedly low or modest libido among women is increasingly seen as a 'medical' problem to be solved pharmacologically. In addition, surgical procedures designed to enhance sexual attractiveness or performance are increasingly being promoted and sought by both sexes for cosmetic reasons – above and below the waist. If one runs with the economic logic, the 'product' is undergoing further product design, being perfected and made more widely and instantly available.

The commodification of sex is big business, which ranges over a number of overlapping spheres of activity, markets and business enterprises, all of which have their political, cultural and, fundamentally, economic dynamics. Sexual desire and demand is stimulated, even 'educated' through advertising and marketing; through allied industries like fashion or tourism; and through the conduits of popular culture – television, magazines, blogs, chatrooms etc. Sex sells, but in selling cars, razors and perfumes by way of association, sex itself is promoted as a commodity. In this chapter I shall attempt to provide a brief overview of this economy of distorted desire, reflecting on its implications for persons and communities, beginning with the most overt and brutal form of sexual commodification – the trade in bodies.

## The body . . . and soul trade

In the last thirty years there has been a significant increase in the demand for international prostitution, partly as a result of mass tourism and partly because of the numbers of men serving the military, UN or even NGOs abroad. This has generated a highly profitable market in the sale of women and children for sexual exploitation. Sold, kidnapped or deceived, hundreds of thousands of women and children are trafficked each year within, or increasingly between, nations and put to work as prostitutes, strippers, or as performers in the production of pornography or live sex shows.

It is impossible to provide accurate estimates of the global number of those involved in this modern sexual slavery. The US Department of Justice estimates that 600,000–800,000 people are trafficked each year, of which 70 per cent are females destined for sexual exploitation. This brutal, inhumane and highly lucrative trade (worth between $5 billion and $7 billion worldwide) proceeds briskly along well-known trade routes, characteristically from the poor rural hinterlands to the richer cities and tourist hot-spots. In broad terms, the USA, Western Europe and Japan 'import', while South America, Africa, Asia and Eastern Europe 'export'. However, even within the same geographical region there is extensive movement: from Burma and Northern Thailand to the tourist-rich south; from Thailand to Japan where the prevalence of Thai sex workers has resulted in certain urban areas being dubbed 'Little Bangkoks'; from Nepal to the brothels of North India; and from Albania, Moldova, Romania and the Ukraine to the cities of Western Europe, where Eastern European girls characteristically make up three-quarters of the prostitute population.

Like any other business, 'supply' and 'demand' shifts with broader changes in the economy and in regulatory regimes. So, for example, prostitution and child trafficking has increased significantly in Vietnam since it opened up to the West and embraced market reforms. Similarly, increased prosperity in China has led to a surge in girls brought from Vietnam, Cambodia and Laos to serve the new expanding market, a market fed by the traditional Chinese belief that sex with a virgin makes a man young again.

Enforced or bonded prostitution is now an integral and fast-growing element in international organized crime. Its victims retained through ongoing intimidation, isolation, rape, drugs, imprisonment or the threat of force bear a horrendous price in terms of physical and psychological health, loss of dignity and well-being. They are habitually sold on several times and cannot expect conditions to improve even when their 'value' in the sex market inevitably declines – with age.

It is important to draw a distinction in principle between those who have been coerced into commercial sex work and those whose engagement is, at some level, chosen. And indeed the work of most of the agencies campaigning against sex trafficking is focused on enhancing the autonomy, and conditions, of sex workers, rather than seeking the abolition of the 'industry'. However, the drawing of lines in such a world is not straightforward. For as law enforcement is strengthened in particular areas, more subtle and indirect forms of coercion and deception emerge.

In purchasing sex, the 'punter', or consumer, is not just buying a service they are also making a payment to limit their responsibility and the consequences of their actions. They are paying to avoid worry about intimacy, reciprocity and any other long-term consequences (including pregnancy). But the 'purity' promised by this commercial relationship is of course illusory: for such neat and convenient boundaries cannot be maintained when sex is treated as a commodity. The consumer and his (or her) desire for sex is part of a global network, for whether they choose to recognize it or not, the 'demand' for sexual services is blind, it stimulates the market irrespective of the supply, be it organized crime or a more 'legitimate' source. But it isn't just the individual punter who is deeply implicated in this web, it is also the tourist industry which facilitates such encounters. For, like the proverbial Russian doll, sex tourism sits hidden within and behind an attractive façade.

## Touching paradise

The tourist is someone who takes time out from the world of work and everyday responsibilities to relax, to be physically refreshed, to escape and, above all, to experience – experience fun, excitement, entertainment, perhaps romance. Tourists have earned their break and often wish to spend their money somewhere else 'away from it all'. Holidaying is a cathartic experience. To assist them, there is a highly developed and

professional industry to sell them 'packages' with abundant opportunities for experiences which emphasis the sights, the sounds, the feelings
of somewhere exotic and sensual. More particularly, the images and the
fantasies conjured of exotic otherness emphasize the body as a source
of pleasure. The tourist experience encourages the suspension of normal
mores in an environment that also places great emphasis on the authorized purchase of pleasure. In this fantastic world, sex is a natural sequel
to sun, sand and surf. A reality strongly reinforced by the extensive sexual
imagery employed in tourism advertising.

Certain destinations have long been marketed more explicitly for
sexual tourism. Indeed several countries, most obviously Thailand,
have come to depend upon sex tourists, directly and indirectly, as a
source of foreign exchange and employment. It is integral to economic
development. One estimate suggests that it accounts for 13 per cent of
GNP (Seager 2003). But such developments need to be seen in a
broader economic and political context. Sex tourism in Thailand has its
origins in the Vietnam War and the provision of recreational facilities
to US troops based in Thailand. This arrangement was formalized by
an agreement signed by the Thai government in 1967. The subsequent
expansion and legitimation of a range of forms of 'entertainment' based
on this political and military foundation transformed the indigenous
patterns of prostitution, creating an 'industry' serving foreigners. As a
tourist destination, then, especially throughout the 1980s and 1990s,
Thailand attracted and catered for a particularly high number of single
males from Australia, Japan, Europe and the USA.

Undoubtedly part of the appeal of the Far East has been the development of a certain image, rooted in Victorian ideas about the Orient,
that Thai and other 'eastern' girls are 'exotic, pliable, sexually innocent
but fun-loving' (Ryan and Hall 2001, p. 12). Furthermore, there is the
cultural perception that such fun-lovers might well play by different
moral rules, for they are unencumbered by the puritanical heritage of
Christianity. Therefore it is 'all right'.

Of course, it is not just Thai women who are commodified and
objectified, sexual tourism can be found increasingly across the globe
with varying degrees of formality and organization. Equally it is not just
men who enter the sexual marketplace cash in hand for there are plenty
of western females seeking to 'rent a dread' in Jamaica or experience
the company of the beach boys of Barbados, Gambia or Bali.

Traditionally, sex tourism has been invisible; dependent upon the exercise of confidentiality and discretion it has existed, as much explicit
sex activity has, on the margins, in the realm of the private. However,
in the last twenty years or so that has changed quite significantly
with the advent of explicitly marketed 'sex holidays'. Perhaps the most

notorious of these has been Club 18–30, which has explicitly encouraged sexual adventurism within its purpose-built compounds. But it is not alone, for like all businesses the leisure industry is diversifying with niche markets springing up to cater for particular needs and age groups. In the 1990s, Hedonism resorts have sprung up in Jamaica and Brazil, attracting a slightly older and wealthier demographic (30–45 years) and a much higher proportion of women (Hawkes 2004). The visibility and ambiguities of such enterprises juxtaposing rich, white tourists from North America and Europe and local black staff who service such sexual playgrounds has even served as the subject matter for the French novelist Michel Houellebecq, who explores its cultural and economic logic in his novel *Plateforme* (Platform).

Leisure developments like Hedonism are a long way from the donkey rides and sand castles of the beaches of Blackpool or Scarborough, and provide a notable example of the dissolution of a once clear distinction drawn between the private world, where explicit sex might occur (most obviously in brothels), and the sphere of public 'decency'. But how did society move from there to here?

# From 'under the counter' to erotic retailing

In the early post-war period, sex shops were few in number and like brothels and strip clubs tucked away in a handful of locations, most notably Soho. However, the introduction of the Obscene Publications Act in 1959 marked the beginning of a process of liberalization that was rapidly accelerated by the profound cultural shift of the 1960s. With the supply of explicit printed material and films significantly increased, not least by the removal of prohibitions on pornography in Denmark and then Sweden, a small number of sex entrepreneurs exploited the new opportunities for nationwide distribution of pornography. Sex shops with their shuttered windows and rather seedy image spread throughout the larger towns in the 1970s. Parallel to these retail outlets clearly aimed at a male clientele was the Ann Summers chain with its exotic lingerie, contraceptives and sex aids aimed at women.

Despite significant growth during the 1970s and 1980s the 'adult entertainment' sector of the economy remained separate – it required people to enter and exit through doors marked 'Private', 'Adult only', or furtively to reach to the top shelf for 'dirty' magazines. Perhaps unsurprisingly then the most successful marketing development of the 1980s was also firmly within the sphere of the private, namely the Ann Summers party, which became a more successful venue for marketing its products than the shops themselves.

All this changed in the 1990s, when much more explicit sexual imagery began to appear on television, in advertising and in mainstream magazines. Alongside such changes there was a rapid expansion of female erotica with sex toys, lingerie, erotic books, DVDs and videos aimed explicitly at women, largely by women – stimulated by developments in the mainstream media which deliberately sought to push the boundaries, including TV series like *Sex and the City* and *Sex Tips for Girls*. Critically these changes have not been veiled behind window shutters or hidden away in private homes – far from it. Located at the very centre of popular culture, they have generated much discussion and shaped attitudes. Perhaps emblematic of the shift over a generation was the fact that Sam Roddick, the daughter of the woman who founded the Body Shop, opened her own retail outlet in 2001 in fashionable Covent Garden, Coco de Mer, one of a number of up-market erotic emporia.

The development of such erotic retailing explicitly aimed at women is of profound significance for two reasons. The first is that it effectively removes much of the cultural opposition to a lot of the 'adult entertainment industry': throughout the 1970s and 1980s an uneasy alliance existed between traditional faith groups and many feminists, the latter opposed to pornography and sex shops primarily on the premise that it exploited and objectified women, making them the passive victims of male, and misogynist, fantasies, including fantasies of rape. Central to this opposition was the issue of power: pornography robbed women of their own autonomy as sexual persons and encouraged unhealthy fantasies among men, linking power and control to sex. Obviously the fact that pornography and sexual products were no longer the exclusive domain of the sleazy male, but designed, produced and marketed by, and for, women has completely undermined this argument.

Second, erotic retailing is 'softly' marketed. It links the playful exploration of sexuality into the world of fashion and lifestyling: so, for example, some 'porno-chic' products are marketed in the designer range (with a price tag to match), others are aimed at 'John Lewis tastes' (Attwood 2005). These associations are supported by extensive discussion about sexual practices in women's magazines and indeed well beyond, most notably in the stream of highly explicit sexual autobiographies and diaries, including *Girl with a One Track Mind*, the result of a popular blog site.

Unsurprisingly, in this more open and democratic world of sexual consumerism, the selling of services and products is couched primarily in terms of the emancipation, empowerment and enhancement of female autonomy. Doubtless for many, the sense of sexual empowerment and self-confidence gained has made a genuinely positive contribution to enhancing the quality of their intimate and lifelong relationships. And were such erotic marketing to be an unambiguous indication that coercive and exploitative sexual practices were a thing of the past, there would be much to celebrate. But there are significant reasons for concern.

Despite the 'soft sell', erotic retailing operates as a bridge between the world of fashion, lifestyle and identity and the 'old world' of male pornography. It therefore helps to dissolve the stigma attached to pornography and other forms of the commercialization of sex. Erotic retailing is thus fully integrated into a world that until recently lurked on the edges of social acceptability (e.g. sado-masochism, swinging, voyeurism, fetishism). With the rise of the Internet, anyone and everyone with a computer and modem can in the privacy of their own rooms receive an unlimited and unregulated supply of pornographic stimulation. Thus the commercial exploitation of sexual desire has well and truly emerged from the 'underground', is percolating into people's homes and lives and is readjusting the boundaries of what is normal within wider culture. Inevitably, the vocabulary, aesthetics and practices of traditional pornography are not just entering the heads, but influencing the habits of ordinary adults – and adolescents. In short, we are undergoing a 'pornification' of culture. As one teenage girl interviewed for an article in the *Observer*, discussing her sexual experience, put it: 'I don't even know what my vocabulary would be if I hadn't seen porn' (Aitkenhead 2006).

## NATSAL 2000

Strong evidence that significant change in actual sexual behaviour has taken place in the last decade or so is provided by the National Survey of Sexual Attitudes and Lifestyles (NATSAL), conducted first in 1990 and then a decade later in 2000. Over 10,000 men and women aged 16–44 were interviewed in each of these detailed surveys. Of particular concern are those areas where behavioural change has been greatest over this single decade. The first of these is in the increase in the number of heterosexual partnerships over a lifetime. This increased significantly for both sexes with higher rates among the younger age groups. The increase was particularly marked for women. In 1990 the 'average' woman in the survey admitted to 3.7 sexual partners in her lifetime – this increased to 6.5 in the year 2000: a massive increase and a clear indication of the 'levelling up' of the traditional 'double standard'.

The second significant change was in the increase in men and women reporting heterosexual anal intercourse in the past year, from 6.5 per cent (7.0) to 11.3 per cent (12.3) for women (men). Let me be clear, I am not passing moral judgement on this particular sexual practice, merely suggesting that its rapid increase is likely to be the result of the process I have described above as 'pornification', that is, the increasing acceptability and normality of a sexual practice as a result of the spread of pornography.

A third significant change has been in the proportion of men paying for sex (i.e. visiting prostitutes). This has increased from 2.1 per cent of the population to 4.3 per cent (Johnson *et al.* 2001). In the context of the increased sexual permissiveness, this may seem a counter-intuitive development. However, it is entirely consistent with the broader picture of the commercialization of sexuality. A culture which encourages sexual exhibitionism in reality TV shows and increasingly licenses sexual excess, for example at stag weekends and hen parties, is one in which barriers to, and the stigma of, paying for sex have been significantly removed.

## Persons and the 'right ordering of desire'

The laissez-faire creed that permeates contemporary culture is a simple one: whatever consenting adults get up to within certain constraints is their business, and theirs alone. Such an amoral stance is entirely consistent with what might be described as an economic model of human nature: people are autonomous, rational, independent individuals who express desires and preferences and seek to realize them. Individuals may co-operate when it is to their advantage, but ultimately they seek to meet their own needs. Thus if they experience sexual desire, that desire can be gratified in a range of ways depending on their preference and of course their ability to get what they want. In this reductive model sexuality has one clear end – pleasure, achieved by the exercise of a short-term consumer preference.

This economic model of sexuality is rendered culturally plausible by an accompanying rhetoric of freedom and autonomy and indeed it receives a certain imprimatur from the public intellectual and eminent sociologist Anthony Giddens. For, in his book *The Transformation of Intimacy*, Giddens argues that we are witnessing the 'final liberation for sexuality, which thence can become wholly a quality of individuals and their transactions with one another' (Giddens 1992, p. 43). Having previously been tied through its procreative function to the institution of marriage as proscribed by a Christian culture and nurtured by the ideal of romantic love, sexuality has now been set free. It has become the 'property' of the free and equal autonomous individual, male or female, and can be deployed as he or she sees fit. Relationships are entered into, and sustained (for as long as they are maintained), only in so far as they meet the needs, desires or current 'life projects' of the individual concerned. Consistent with this, Giddens finds some merit in one-night stands: 'even in the shape of impersonal, fleeting contacts, episodic sexuality may be a positive form of everyday experiment' (Giddens 1992, p. 147).

Yet, clearly economic exchange is only part of what we engage in as humans: the market but one (albeit powerful) sphere of our social world. To the thoughtful student of life, therefore, Christian or otherwise, the account of human nature, sexual desire and relationships sketched above seems somewhat simplistic and naive. Yet, given its prevalence, it is perhaps worth sketching out some of the inadequacies with this understanding of the nature of human desire, sexual acts, personhood and, indeed, what constitutes freedom.

One of the fundamental problems is inherent to the marketing of sexual gratification and the objectification of sex. For if it is treated as an end in itself, sexual desire cannot simply be satiated, it is restless and, in the absence of moral or other forms of restraint, it seeks new experiences and novelties to maintain the same level of stimulation. In short, when separated from a relationship with some emotional content, it operates like a drug. So, for example, the vast majority of sex tourists who use child prostitutes are not exclusively interested in children, rather they are first and foremost users of prostitutes, who have moved on to newer pastures (Ryan and Hall 2001). In this respect, casual anonymous sexual encounters between consenting adults and the worst abuses of forced prostitution can be seen as existing on the same spectrum: there is a natural affinity between all sexual behaviours which share the characteristic of objectifying others for the purposes of sexual gratification.

The second difficulty relates to the fact that contractual relationships are designed to limit risk and constrict the character of the exchange between persons so that there are few if any consequences. Thus while friendship may operate on a free flow of give and take, in the market the nature of an exchange is rational, explicit and occurs simultaneously. The fundamental problem with human sexual desire is that it simply doesn't fit this model. Sexual experience inevitably generates psychological and emotional consequences. These may be denied, repressed, ignored, but ultimately human sexual encounters can only 'fit' into a commercial model through being distorted. This distortion means that much that passes for 'sex' in such an economy requires active pretence and the construction of artificial fantasy for, both punter and prostitute. Such a fantasy economy short-changes the human person. The nature of much 'sex' that is 'had' is thus fragmentary, because it is not between whole persons.

Ironically it is sometimes the body itself that is missing in many contemporary sexual encounters. For in the case of sex chatlines, the flickering computer screen or even scrolling text (e.g. with cyber-sex), a reduced number of the dominant senses (visual, auditory) are stimulated in the context of solitary sexual activity to produce a brief moment of pleasure and relief of sexually generated tension. One of the distortions of such 'bodiless' sex is the illusion that bodies do not really matter at all. For it assumes that we *have* bodies, rather like we *have* cars, instead of acknowledging that we *are* bodies. As such, it strives to maintain the illusion that whatever we may choose to do with our body is of little consequence, as if our 'real' self existed purely in our (compartmentalized) mental life.

Of course the most fundamental dimension missing in the objectified sexual encounter is the recognition of an authentic encounter between persons; rather, such encounters are 'staged' and participants 'act out' their parts. Yet sexual acts and patterns of sexual behaviour contribute significantly to our formation as human beings. Even the briefest of sexual episodes can have consequences; sexual encounters cannot be completely 'purified' of their broader human context. Anonymous sex therefore blunts and limits the participant's capacity to be human, and one of the ironies of sexual objectification is that the emphasis on the explicit, and indeed the efficient, makes it the antithesis of the erotic.

Finally, there is the matter of freedom, autonomy and choice – or at least the illusion of these. Many of those who advocate or commend sexual freedom seem strangely unaware of the fact that humans are deeply social in character and receive much of their sense of value and self-worth from their interactions with others: others in-form and in-fluence who we are and who we will become. A culture that promotes the sexual objectification of others creates expectations and pressures upon individuals to conform. Children and adolescents are particularly vulnerable to such expectations. They do not exist hermetically sealed away from the constant bombardment of images and ideas through television and the Internet, and the power of what is 'normal' informs the processes of adolescent identity formation at exactly the point at which sexual feelings emerge. Children are not able to grow up in a world devoid of such powerful influences; rather they are subjected to forces that would seek their premature sexualization. One of the particularly sad aspects of the NATSAL 2000 findings is the high proportion of teenagers, especially girls, who regret their first sexual experience and feel it took place as a result of peer pressure or alcohol (Wellings *et al.* 2001).

## Conclusion

For the Christian there are no short cuts to true human fulfilment: it certainly isn't achieved through the simple pursuit of bodily desire. Rather it rests upon the quality and rightness of our relationships with others, from love of neighbour – and of God. Other people cannot simply be treated as objects, however willing, for our gratification, without harm-ful consequences. They demand dignity and respect, even, or perhaps especially, when they fail to seek it for themselves. The body's sexual-ity is not then a trivial matter, its expression constitutes a gift of the self to another and for that gift to be properly received a relationship is required where there is mutual reciprocity. This in turn requires the establish-ment and building of trust over time. And trust, by its very nature, involves people taking risks with one another, opening themselves up, making themselves vulnerable. This requires time and the sort of faithful com-mitment traditionally associated with marriage. The unconditional public commitment of marriage, 'for better, for worse, for richer, for poorer, in sickness and in health' provides a certain freedom for rela-tionships 'to "take time" to mature and become as profoundly nurturing as they can' (Williams 2002, p. 315). It is exactly this freedom that is being eroded by the onslaught of a sexualized culture with its rich but empty world of choice.

Within marriage, sexual desire is then subordinated to a greater task: it is ordered, and put to work in the service of the marriage relationship. In particular, it is envisaged that it will express and strengthen the mar-riage bond and result in children who can be loved and nurtured within a clear framework. But the right ordering of sexuality is also about the acceptance of limits and boundaries. It involves a discipline of desire set in the context of a faithful, exclusive and permanent relationship that is radically at odds with a culture in which sexuality is trivialized and objectified. Indeed some of the language of the 1662 BCP Marriage Service, which warns of 'men's carnal lusts and appetites, like brute beasts that have no understanding', describes aspects of our current culture fairly accurately.

Current discussions within the Church about the legitimacy of same-sex relationships are taking place in the context of what is effectively a cultural war over the meaning of sexuality and the implications of the body. On one side is an understanding of sexuality that tends to reduce its nature to the purely hedonistic. Conceiving of it as a posses-sion of the individual, it is easily co-opted by the logic of consumerism that dominates our society. On the other side is a more multifaceted understanding of sexuality, which argues that it must be subordinated to 'higher' ends and oriented to the common good through the dis-ciplines associated with a public commitment to relationships marked by faithfulness, exclusivity and permanence. In light of the profound nature of this fault-line it seems therefore somewhat perverse for some Christians to oppose the request from others that they might be permitted to seek the imposition of such a counter-cultural discipline and public commitment upon their same-sex relationships.

# References

Ackman, D., 'How Big is porn?' http://www.forbes.com/2001/05/25/0524porn.html. Accessed 09/03/2006.

Aitkenhead, D., 'Sex, now', *Guardian Weekend*, April 15, 2006.

Attwood, F., 'Fashion and passion: marketing sex to women', *Sexualities* 8.4, 2005, 392–406.

Bellis, M. A. *et al.*, 'Sexual behaviour of young people in international tourist resorts', *Sex. Transm. Infect* 80, 2004, 43–7.

Giddens, A., *The Transformation of Intimacy: Sexuality, Love and Eroticism in Modern Societies*, Polity Press, Cambridge, 1992.

Hawkes, G., *Sex and Pleasure in Western Culture*, Polity Press, Cambridge, 2004.

Houellebecq, M., *Platform*, Vintage, London, 2003.

Johnson, A. M. *et al.*, 'Sexual behaviour in Britain: partnerships, practices, and HIV risk behaviours', *The Lancet* 358, 2001, 1835–42.

Ryan, C. and Hall, C. M., *Sex Tourism: Marginal People and Liminalities*, Routledge, London, 2001.

Scholsser, E., *Reefer Madness and Other Tales from the American Underground*, Penguin, London, 2003.

Seager, J., *The Penguin Atlas of Women in the World*, Penguin, London, 2003.

Wellings, K. *et al.*, 'Sexual behaviour in Britain: early heterosexual experience', *The Lancet* 358, 2001, 1843–50.

Williams, R., 'The body's grace' in *Theology and Sexuality: Classic and Contemporary Readings*, ed. E. F. Rogers, Blackwell, Oxford, 2002.

# Afterword: listening in the pews

DUNCAN DORMOR AND JEREMY MORRIS

In 1991, the House of Bishops produced their statement *Issues in Human Sexuality*. Its purpose was to 'promote an educational process as a result of which Christians may both become more informed about and understanding of certain human realities, and also enter more deeply into the wisdom of their inheritance of faith in this field' (para. 1.9). Unfortunately, while *Issues in Human Sexuality* is widely cited, it is often used to end or foreclose discussion rather than start it. Sadly, this is indicative of a broader tendency within Anglican Christianity, where the 'debate' about the place of gay Christians has often lacked exactly those characteristics that would make it fruitful: a humble disposition, attentive listening, prayerful exploration and engaged conversation. To the distress of many ordinary Christians (and doubtless many church leaders), pleas that we might become, as a Christian community, seekers after information, understanding and even wisdom have all too often been drowned out by more shrill and rancorous voices. The 'gay' debate has not exactly been the place to look for evidence that Christians might be known for their 'love for one another' (John 13.35).

We have written this book mindful of the need for a more genuinely educational process. We have therefore attempted to think through the issue of homosexuality using the traditional Anglican threefold recourse to scripture, tradition and reason. Clearly and explicitly acknowledging that we stand under the authority of scripture within the moral and historical community of faith that is the Church, we have tried to be realistic and honest about the complexity of the task before us all and steer clear of the polemic or rhetoric which has marked, or marred, so much of this debate. Indeed, we are as interested and concerned to provoke thought about *how* we think and argue together as Anglicans drawing on the resources of scripture, tradition and reason as we are to cast some light (if we have) upon this contested issue. In so doing we have sought to present some of the complexity and ambiguities involved in the difficult business of biblical interpretation and indeed in the recourse to 'tradition' as a source of authority for the Church today. All too often, contemporary Christian reflection tends to present a sanitized or idealized account of the past.

Our hope then has been to produce a book which will prompt thinking and raise questions rather than provide clear answers. This more open-ended approach will doubtless frustrate many. But it is quite deliberate, and we hope that there will be some readers who gain from reading the book without necessarily agreeing with us that practising gay Christians, lay or ordained, can indeed play a full and publicly recognized part in every aspect of our church life.

In the course of *An Acceptable Sacrifice?* we have covered a good deal of terrain both historically and geographically, and particularly in the last section we have stressed the importance of global factors, but when all is said and done the test of Christian discipleship, of the love that we bear one another, is most tangible at the level of the local parish and congregation. For there is an intimacy about life within the Christian community that is inescapable: we are after all 'brothers and sisters in Christ' and we share not just the scriptures and the richness of the Christian tradition as a whole, but also the particular experience of what it means to worship and belong within a local Christian community. Here our sense of being fellow travellers and companions in faith is deepened by a more intimate history of involvement with particular people. We are implicated in the lives and experiences of other Christians who may quite literally be our neighbours or, if not, fellow members of the choir, PCC or youth group. Worshipping with others in the pew involves us, to some degree, in their lives, their joys and sorrows, their triumphs, even perhaps something of their difficult times. Inevitably, such knowledge includes something of the relationships they have with others. We may know that their husband only visits at Christmas and Easter, how hard they saved to buy their house, that their grown-up son suffers from bad bouts of depression or that their daughter now lives in Cardiff.

Just like anyone else, gay Christians worship and pray as part of local congregations. That a person is gay and lives with their partner is then potentially part of that 'congregational knowledge' shared in fellowship and prayer. In some Christian communities the public acknowledgement that a person is gay is unremarkable; they are simply accepted for who they are, indeed the history of their relationship may be known and remarked upon in the same way as that of a married couple. In others, however, public acknowledgement that a person is gay, irrespective of whether they are in a relationship or not, is a deeply threatening form of knowledge and a source of anxiety for the congregation and its leadership. If the person in question seeks acceptance on their own terms, they may indeed become a 'problem' that in practice is only resolved by their departure. Perhaps inevitably, those gay Christians who do not respond to their rejection by fellow Christians by leaving the church, tend to gravitate towards churches that accept them. So the Church finds itself in a Catch-22 situation which can exacerbate discussions between what might broadly be described as 'conservatives' and 'liberals'. From their experience the former may believe that gay Christians are 'thin on the ground' and the few they encounter strident advocates asserting their rights, whereas the latter, whose knowledge of gay Christians may be bound up with knowledge of their faith commitment, hospitality and life-stories are unable to recognize the picture of 'gay people' painted by some traditionalists.

For the Christian, love of God in Christ Jesus cannot be separated from love of our neighbour. As the House of Bishops recognized in 1991,

> The story of the Church's attitude to homosexuals has too often been one of prejudice, ignorance and oppression. All of us need to acknowledge that, and to repent for any part we may have had in it. The Church has begun to listen . . . and must deepen and extend that listening.

There are many places within the Church where that process of listening and engagement has yet to begin in earnest. Yet if our love for our gay brother or sister is to be genuine and sincere, it is our starting point. Perhaps it is only from that encounter that we will begin to form a clear and hopeful answer to the question, 'How is the gospel good news if you're gay?'

# Further reading

### Introduction (Duncan Dormor and Jeremy Morris)

House of Bishops, *Issues in Human Sexuality: A Statement by the House of Bishops*, Church House Publishing, London, 1991.

House of Bishops Group, *Some Issues in Human Sexuality: A Guide to the Debate*, A discussion document from the House of Bishops Group on *Issues in Human Sexuality*, Church House Publishing, London, 2003.

The Lambeth Commission on Communion, *The Windsor Report 2004*, Anglican Consultative Council, London, 2004.

### 1 Whose text is it anyway? (Maggi Dawn)

Adam, Andrew, *What Is Postmodern Biblical Criticism?* Guides to Biblical Scholarship New Testament Series, Fortress Press, Minneapolis, 1995.

Green, Garrett, *Theology, Hermeneutics, and Imagination: The Crisis of Interpretation at the End of Modernity*, Cambridge University Press, Cambridge, 1999.

Vanhoozer, Kevin, *Is there a Meaning in this Text? The Bible, the Reader, and the Morality of Literary Knowledge*, Zondervan, Grand Rapids, 1998.

### 2 Threat and promise (Andrew Mein)

Barton, John, *Ethics and the Old Testament*, SCM Press, London, 1998.

Gagnon, Robert and Via, Dan, *Homosexuality and the Bible: Two Views*, Fortress Press, Minneapolis, 2003.

Moore, Gareth, *A Question of Truth: Christianity and Homosexuality*, Continuum, London, 2003.

Nissinen, Martti, *Homoeroticism in the Biblical World: A Historical Perspective*, Fortress Press, Minneapolis, 1998.

### 3 The call of Christ (Arnold Browne)

Balch, David (ed.), *Homosexuality, Science, and the 'Plain Sense' of Scripture*, Eerdmans, Grand Rapids, 2000.

Countryman, William, *Dirt, Greed and Sex: Sexual Ethics in the NT and their Implications for Today*, SCM Press, London, 1989.

Gagnon, Robert, *The Bible and Homosexual Practice: Texts and Hermeneutics*, Abingdon Press, Nashville, 2001.

Meeks, Wayne, *The Origins of Christian Morality: The First Two Centuries*, Yale University Press, New Haven, 1993.

Radcliffe, Timothy, 'Paul and Sexual Identity: 1 Corinthians 11.2–16' in Janet. Soskice (ed.), *After Eve: Women, Theology and the Christian Tradition*, Marshall Pickering, London, 1990.

## 4 The Church and change (Jeremy Morris)

Avis, Paul, *The Anglican Understanding of the Church: An Introduction*, SPCK, London, 2000.
Newman, John H., *An Essay on the Development of Christian Doctrine* (1845), many editions subsequently, including Penguin, London, 1974.
Redfern, Alistair, *Being Anglican*, Darton, Longman & Todd, London, 2000.
Ross White, Stephen, *Authority and Anglicanism*, SCM Press, London, 1996.
Thompson, Michael, *When Should We Divide?* Grove Books, Cambridge, 2004.

## 5 Godly conversation (Jessica Martin)

Carlson, Eric, *Marriage and the English Reformation*, Blackwell, Oxford, 1994.
Cressy, David, *Birth, Marriage and Death: Ritual, Religion and the Life Cycle in Tudor and Stuart England*, Oxford University Press, Oxford, 1997.
MacCulloch, Diarmaid, *Thomas Cranmer*, Yale University Press, New Haven and London, 1996.

## 6 Friends, companions and bedfellows (Duncan Dormor)

Boswell, James, *The Marriage of Likeness*, HarperCollins, London, 1995.
Bray, Alan, *The Friend*, University of Chicago Press, Chicago, 2003.
Bray, Alan, *Homosexuality in Renaissance England*, Columbia University Press, Colombia, 1996.
Hitchcock, Tim, *English Sexualities 1700–1800*, Macmillan, London, 1997.

## 7 Thinking about Christ's body (Jessica Martin)

Nouwen, Henri, *Clowning in Rome: Reflections on Solitude, Celibacy, Prayer*, Darton, Longman & Todd, London, 2001.
Williams, Rowan, 'Is there a Christian sexual ethic?' in *Open to Judgement: Sermons and Addresses*, Darton, Longman & Todd, London, 1994.

## 8 'Neither male nor female' (John Hare)

Coxon, Anthony, 'Understanding sexual diversity' in Andrew Linzey and Richard Kirker (eds), *Gays and the Future of Anglicanism*, John Hunt, Ropley, 2005.
Edmonds, D. Keith, 'Sexual differentiation – normal and abnormal' in Robert Shaw, W. Soutter and Stuart Stanton (eds), *Gynaecology*, Churchill, London, 1992.

## 9 Psychology and orientation (Arnold Browne)

Brooten, Bernadette, *Love between Women: Early Christian Responses to Female Homoeroticism*, Chicago University Press, Chicago, 1996.
Dollimore, Jonathan, *Sexual Dissidence: Augustine to Wilde, Freud to Foucault*, Clarendon Press, Oxford, 1991.
Skinner, Marilyn. *Sexuality in Greek and Roman Culture*, Blackwell, Oxford, 2005.

## 10 Sex and the city (Malcolm Brown)

Atherton, John, *Christianity and the Market: Christian Social Thought for Our Times*, SPCK, London, 1992.

Jenkins, David, *Market Whys and Human Wherefores: Thinking Again about Markets, Politics and People*, Cassell, London, 2000.

Hay, Donald and Kreider, Alan, *Christianity and the Culture of Economics*, University of Wales Press, Cardiff, 2001.

Moe-Lobeda, Cynthia, *Healing a Broken World: Globalization and God*, Fortress Press, Minneapolis, 2002.

## 11 HIV/AIDS (Michael Beasley)

Foster, Geoff, Levine, Carol and Williamson, John (eds), *A Generation at Risk: The Global Impact of HIV and AIDS on Orphans and Vulnerable Children*, Cambridge University Press, Cambridge, 2005.

Keenan, James (ed.), *Catholic Ethicists on HIV/AIDS Prevention*, Continuum, New York, 2000.

Stillwaggon, Eileen, *AIDS and the Ecology of Poverty*, Oxford University Press, Oxford, 2005.

## 12 Selling body and soul (Duncan Dormor)

Coelho, Paulo, *Eleven Minutes*, HarperCollins, London, 2003.

Houellebecq, Michel, *Platform*, Vintage, London, 2003.

Johnson, Anne *et al.*, 'Sexual behaviour in Britain: partnerships, practices, and HIV risk behaviours'. *The Lancet* 358, 2001, 1835–42.

Rogers, Eugene, *Sexuality and the Christian Body*, Blackwell, Oxford, 1999.

Ryan, Chris and Hall, Mike, *Sex Tourism: Marginal People and Liminalities*, Routledge, London, 2001.

Williams, Rowan. 'The body's grace' in *Theology and Sexuality: Classic and Contemporary Readings*, ed. Eugene Rogers, Blackwell, Oxford, 2002.

# Index of biblical references

# Index of subjects

CPSIA information can be obtained
at www.ICGtesting.com
Printed in the USA
BVHW041450160322
631623BV00007B/112